OCR GCSE

History A
Schools History Project

Crime & Punishment Through Time

Johannes Ahrenfelt   Neal Watkin

www.heinemann.co.uk
✓ Free online support
✓ Useful weblinks
✓ 24 hour online ordering

01865 888080

OCR
RECOGNISING ACHIEVEMENT   Heinemann
Official Publisher Partnership

Heinemann is an imprint of Pearson Education Limited, a company incorporated in England and Wales, having its registered office at Edinburgh Gate, Harlow, Essex, CM20 2JE. Registered company number: 872828

www.heinemann.co.uk

Heinemann is a registered trademark of Pearson Education Limited

Text © Pearson Education Limited 2009

First published 2009

13 12 11 10 09
10 9 8 7 6 5 4 3 2 1

British Library Cataloguing in Publication Data
A catalogue record for this book is available from the British Library

ISBN 978 0 4350145 7

Edited by Elaine Corke
Proofread by Dodi Beardshaw
Designed by Pearson Education Limited
Project managed and typeset by Wearset Ltd, Boldon, Tyne and Wear
Original illustrations © Pearson Education Limited 2009
Illustrated by Wearset Ltd, Boldon, Tyne and Wear
Cover design by Pearson Education Limited
Picture research by Q2AMedia
Cover photo/illustration © Getty Images/Stone
Printed in the UK by Scotprint

Acknowledgements
The author and publisher would like to thank the following individuals and organisations for permission to reproduce copyright material:

Page 2 Source A Copyright Guardian News & Media Ltd 2002. **Page 6 Source B** Maureen Duffy *England: The Making of the Myth from Stonehenge to Albert* Fourth Estate Ltd 2001. **Page 9 Source C** Sheppard, Sunderland and Frere *A History of Roman Britain* Routledge 1987. **Page 9 Source D** Sheppard, Sunderland and Frere *A History of Roman Britain* Routledge 1987. **Page 23 Source B** Maureen Duffy *England: The Making of the Myth from Stonehenge to Albert* Fourth Estate Ltd 2001. **Page 26 Source A** J. A. Guy *Oxford History of Britain* Oxford University Press 1992. By permission of Oxford University Press. **Page 27 Source G** Material from Internet Shakespeare Editions, The University of Victoria and Social Sciences and Humanities Research Council of Canada (http://internetshakespeare.uvic.ca). **Page 27 Source H** Material from Internet Shakespeare Editions, The University of Victoria and Social Sciences and Humanities Research Council of Canada (http://internetshakespeare.uvic.ca). **Page 28 Source A** P. Ackroyd *Dickens* Mandarin 1991. **Page 35 Source D** C. Emsley *Crime and Society in England 1750–1900* Longman 2004. **Page 35 Source E** C. Bloom *Violent London: 2004 Years of Riots, Rebels and Revolts* Pan Books 2004. **Page 35 Source G** C. Emsley *Crime and Society in England 1750–1900* Longman 2004. **Page 71 Source B** Crown Copyright. National Archives SP 39/19. Part I, f.54–57. **Page 71 Source D** J. Sharpe *Dick Turpin* Profile Books Ltd 2005. **Page 72 Source B** Matthew Taylor 'Homeless DNA taken in begging crackdown' The Guardian 28 February, 2004. **Page 74 Source A** Crown Copyright. Home Office Statistical Bulletin: D. Povey (Ed,) Homicides, Firearm Offences and Intimate Violence 2006/2007. 03/08 31 January 2008. **Page 74 Source B** C. Bloom *Violent London: 2004 Years of Riots, Rebels and Revolts* Pan Books 2004. **Page 74 Source C** C. Emsley *Crime and Society in England 1750–1900* Longman 2004. **Page 80 Source A** J. M. Coutts *Social Issues: Britain* Heinemann Educational Publishers 1985. **Page 81 Source B** Crown Copyright. British Crime Survey 1994. **Page 81 Source D** Stewart Tendler, Crime

Correspondent 'Crime figures show overall fall but violence increases' The Times, 28 September, 1994. **Page 84 Source D** Cecily Hamilton 'The March of the Women'. **Page 86 Source A** Between The Wars Words & Music by Billy Bragg © Copyright 1985 BMG Music Publishing Limited. Universal Music Publishing MGB Limited. Used by permission of Music Sales Limited. All Rights Reserved. International Copyright Secured. **Page 90 Source B** Richard Caseby, Maurice Chittenden, Frances Rafferty, Tim Rayment 'Bloody battle of Trafalgar – London poll tax riot' The Times, 1 April 1990. **Page 90 Source C** Danny Burns, Secretary of the Avon Foundation of the Anti-Poll Tax Unions. **Page 96 Source A** Crown Copyright. National Archives Learning Curve HO 44/18 f.37–48. **Page 98 Source A** Words & Music © Copyright 1953 Karl Dallas/EMI Music. **Page 99 Source B** © Telegraph Media Group Limited 1998. **Page 114 Getting Started** Paul Stokes 'Man is beaten to death chasing car thieves' Daily Telegraph, 2 January, 2002.

The author and publisher would like to thank the following individuals and organisations for permission to reproduce photographs:

Page 8 Jim Young/Reuters. **Page 9** Photograph of Colchester vase reproduced with the kind permission of Colchester and Ipswich Museum Service. **Page 11** Warner Bros. Pictures/TopFoto. **Page 12L** The Art Archive/British Library. **Page 12R** San Vitale, Ravenna, Italy/The Bridgeman Art Library. **Page 13** The Art Archive/British Library. **Page 16** Alfsky/Istockphoto. **Page 19TL** British Library Board. **Page 19M** French School (11th century)/Musee de la Tapisserie, Bayeux, France/ With special authorisation of the city of Bayeux Giraudon/The Bridgeman Art Library. **Page 19TR** Mary Evans Picture Library/Alamy. **Page 19BL** The National Archives of the UK, ref. KB26/223. **Page 19BR** Photodisc/ Phillipe Colombi. **Page 21** Jon Chamberlain/Istockphoto. **Page 24** John Meek/The Art Archive. **Page 27** Hulton Archive/Getty Images. **Page 28** Mary Evans Picture Library. **Page 32T** Mary Evans Picture Library. **Page 32B** English School, (19th century)/Private Collection/The Bridgeman Art Library. **Page 34L** Mary Evans Picture Library. **Page 34R** Mary Evans Picture Library. **Page 35** Mary Evans Picture Library. **Page 36T** Mary Evans Picture Library. **Page 36B** Mary Evans Picture Library. **Page 37** Mary Evans Picture Library. **Page 40** Mary Evans Picture Library. **Page 41** Mary Evans Picture Library. **Page 42** Steven May/Alamy. **Page 46** Dylan Martinez/Reuters. **Page 48** Capital Pictures. **Page 55L** Mary Evans Picture Library. **Page 55TR** Mary Evans Picture Library. **Page 55MR** Master John (fl.1544)/National Portrait Gallery, London, UK/The Bridgeman Art Library. **Page 55 BR** (16th century)/ Private Collection/The Bridgeman Art Library. **Page 61** Mary Evans Picture Library. **Page 62** Mary Evans Picture Library. **Page 66** Mary Evans Picture Library. **Page 68** Mary Evans Picture Library. **Page 70** William Powell Frith. **Page 72** Digital Beach Media/Rex Features. **Page 78** Leech, John (1817–64)/Private Collection/The Bridgeman Art Library. **Page 82** English Photographer (20th century)/Private Collection/The Stapleton Collection/The Bridgeman Art Library. **Page 84** English School, (20th century)/British Library, London, UK/The Bridgeman Art Library. **Page 85** Mary Evans Picture Library. **Page 87** Mary Evans Picture Library. **Page 90** Glyn Howells/Contributor/Getty Images. **Page 92** Associated Press. **Page 101** Associated Press. **Page 103** Mary Evans Picture Library/Photolibrary. **Page 115** Guildhall Library & Art Gallery/Photolibrary. **Page 116** Phil Schermeister/Corbis. **Page 118** Mary Evans Picture Library. **Page 120T** Mary Evans Picture Library. **Page 120B** Mary Evans Picture Library. **Page 124L** (1756–1827) & Pugin, A.C. (1762–1832)/Guildhall Library, City of London/The Bridgeman Art Library. **Page 124R** Mary Evans Picture Library. **Page 125L** Mary Evans Picture Library. **Page 125TR** Mary Evans Picture Library. **Page 125BR** Hulton Archive/Stringer/Getty Images. **Page 126** Mary Evans Picture Library. **Page 137** The Art Archive/British Library. **Page 145** Mary Evans Picture Library. **Page 149** Ashley Cooper/Alamy.

Every effort has been made to contact copyright holders of material reproduced in this book. Any omissions will be rectified in subsequent printings if notice is given to the publishers.

Websites
There are links to relevant websites in this book. In order to ensure that the links are up to date, that the links work, and that the sites are not inadvertently linked to sites that could be considered offensive, we have made the links available on the Heinemann website at www. heinemann.co.uk/hotlinks. When you access the site, the express code is 1457P

Contents

Welcome to OCR History A GCSE (Schools History Project) Crime and Punishment

This book has been written specifically to support you during your OCR GCSE A (SHP) study of the topic Crime and Punishment.

HOW TO USE THIS BOOK

This Crime and Punishment course is a Development Study which means that it investigates how law enforcement, crime and punishment changed or continued across a long period of time. Don't be alarmed, you'll need to have a broad understanding of the main changes and the key factors behind those changes rather than remember everything. You will explore three key themes (see below) which have been divided into five time periods: Roman 500 BC–AD 400, Middle Ages AD 400–1450, Early Modern 1450–1750, Industrial Britain 1750–1900 and The Twentieth Century 1900–2000.

Lots of the lessons begin with a 'Getting Started' activity to encourage you to really think about the content right from the beginning of the lesson.

The activities have been designed to help you understand the specification content and develop your historical skills.

Each lesson has objectives so you know what you will learn and which skills you will be developing in each lesson.

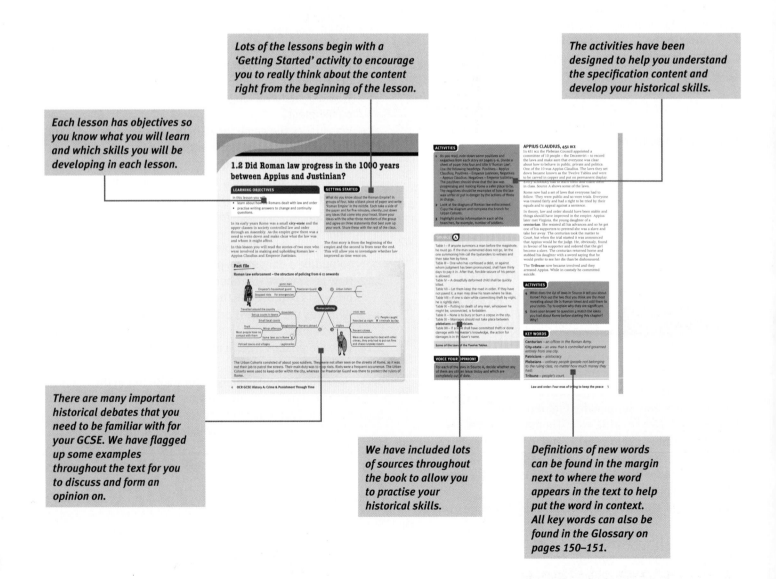

There are many important historical debates that you need to be familiar with for your GCSE. We have flagged up some examples throughout the text for you to discuss and form an opinion on.

We have included lots of sources throughout the book to allow you to practise your historical skills.

Definitions of new words can be found in the margin next to where the word appears in the text to help put the word in context. All key words can also be found in the Glossary on pages 150–151.

In addition to this, you will also find:

HISTORY DETECTIVE

There just is not enough room to include all of the facts in this book so you are going to have to be a detective and find out some for yourself!

FACT FILE!

Fact File boxes contain a list of facts important to the historical context and will help you to develop your knowledge.

HISTORY DETECTIVE

Research the lives and crimes of these other medieval outlaws:
- Eustace the Monk
- Fulk fitzWarin
- Adam de Gurdon

How similar are their stories to the legend of Robin Hood? Do these findings change your view of what medieval crime was actually like?

Fact file

Elizabeth Fry – Born into a Quaker family in Norwich, Elizabeth Fry dedicated her life to helping those less fortunate than herself. After a visit to Newgate Prison, she began a school and Bible group inside the prison in 1817. The following year she gave evidence to a Parliamentary Committee about her work at Newgate.

GRADE STUDIO

Grade Studio is designed for you to improve your chances of achieving the best possible grades.

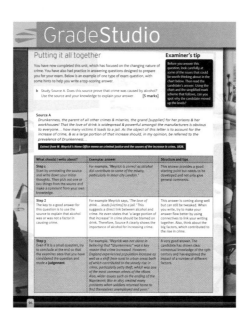

EXAM CAFÉ

The Exam Café is to be used when revising and preparing for exams. The Exam Café could be used in revision classes after school or in revision lessons.

The Exam Café will help you to prepare for the final exam.

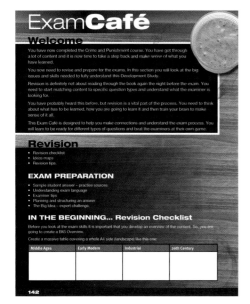

Your BIG STUDY

The main idea behind this study of Crime and Punishment is to allow you to develop the historical skills and knowledge to investigate the **BIG QUESTION**:

> ## Is Britain more violent and crime ridden than ever before?

This will help you find out about the **BIG PICTURE**:

> ## How did crime and punishment change over time?

Which you will do by exploring three **KEY THEMES**:

> ## Crime, Punishment and Law and order

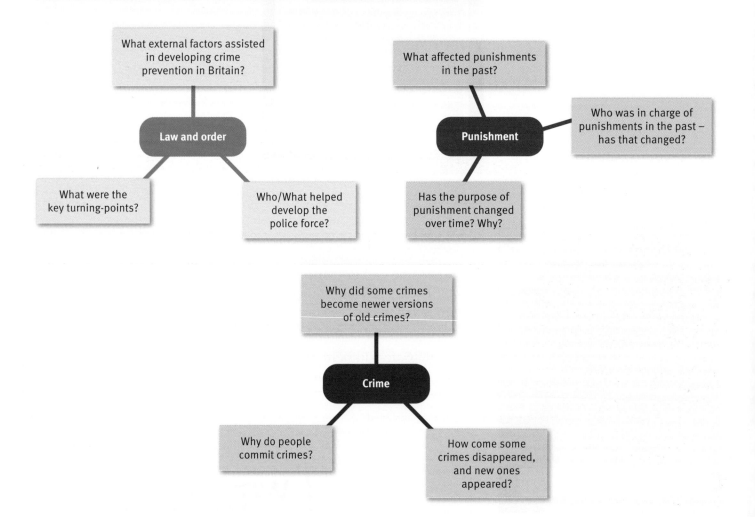

What external factors assisted in developing crime prevention in Britain?

Law and order

What were the key turning-points?

Who/What helped develop the police force?

What affected punishments in the past?

Punishment

Who was in charge of punishments in the past – has that changed?

Has the purpose of punishment changed over time? Why?

Why did some crimes become newer versions of old crimes?

Crime

Why do people commit crimes?

How come some crimes disappeared, and new ones appeared?

How do different factors affect crime and punishment?

Now think about the **BIG FACTORS** below that affect crime and punishment. You will need to come back to these factors throughout the book, particularly during your revision (see Exam Café section pp. 142–9).

For each factor discuss in pairs:

- How does murder affect our opinions about the world we live in; about punishment and policing?
- Is crime becoming more violent? What factors affect the way we view crimes?

- Are punishments too lenient? Did they work when they were harder?
- Should capital punishment be re-introduced?

As you work your way through the book create a table like the one below, perhaps on the last page on your book, or stored on the Virtual Learning Environment so you can add to it for each section of the book. What impact does each factor have on the three Key Themes?

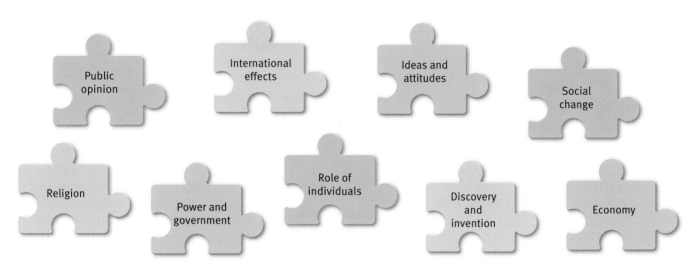

Big factors	Law and order	Crime	Punishment
Power and government			
Religion			
Social change			
Economy			
Public opinion			
Role of individuals			
Ideas and attitudes			
Discovery and invention			
International effects			

Studying Crime and Punishment

The best way of really getting to grips with a Crime and Punishment development study is to analyse a story that deals with many of the issues you will investigate and explore during your GCSE. Source A is one such story.

Stories such as these show many of the aspects that you will be studying in this course: policing and law and order, crime and criminal acts, and punishment and imprisonment. You will need to consider all of these aspects whilst looking through the story.

Six days after the events in Source A, the police arrested Winston Moseley, a 29-year-old business machine operator, and charged him with Kitty Genovese's murder. Moseley also confessed to two other murders while in custody and he was later certified as medically insane. While the accuracy of the reporting of this case has been questioned over the years, the Kitty Genovese case became a symbol of urban indifference and the 'bystander effect'. Winston Moseley was denied parole for his crimes several times including in 2008 when he was 74 years old.

ACTIVITIES

1 Working in pairs, think about the questions that you would like to ask the following people:
   - Assistant Chief Inspector Frederick M. Lussen, the man in charge of the investigation
   - Karl Ross, the witness who first called the police after the final attack
   - Martin Gansberg, the journalist who wrote Source A.
2 Create a 5Ws table with two questions for each 'W' about the 38 witnesses to the event.

   Who? What? When? Why? Where?

   Now discuss your thoughts and questions as a class.

SOURCE A

38 who saw murder didn't call police

For more than half an hour 38 respectable, law-abiding citizens in Queens (New York, USA) watched a killer stalk and stab a woman in three separate attacks in Kew Gardens. Twice the sound of their voices and the sudden glow of their bedroom lights interrupted him and frightened him off. Each time he returned, sought her out and stabbed her again. Not one person telephoned the police during the assault; one witness called after the woman was dead. This is what police say happened beginning at 3:20 a.m.:

Catherine Genovese, who was called Kitty, was returning home from work. At night, this quiet neighborhood is shrouded in the slumbering darkness that marks most residential areas. Miss Genovese noticed a man at the far end of the parking lot. She halted. Then, nervously headed up Austin Street. She got as far as a street light in front of a bookstore before the man grabbed her. She screamed. Lights went on in the ten-story apartment house which faces the bookstore.

Miss Genovese screamed: 'Oh, my God, he stabbed me! Please help me! Please help me!' From one of the upper windows in the apartment house, a man called down: 'Let that girl alone!' The assailant looked up at him, shrugged and walked toward a white sedan parked a short distance away. Miss Genovese struggled to her feet. Lights went out. The killer returned to Miss Genovese, now trying to make her way around the side of the building by the parking lot to get to her apartment. The assailant stabbed her again. 'I'm dying!' she shrieked. 'I'm dying!'

Windows were opened again, and lights went on in many apartments. The assailant got into his car and drove away. Miss Genovese staggered to her feet. A city bus passed by. It was 3:35 a.m. The assailant returned. By then, Miss Genovese had crawled to the back of the building where he saw her slumped on the floor at the foot of the stairs. He stabbed her a third time – fatally.

It was 3:50 a.m. by the time the police received their first call from a man, Karl Ross, who was a neighbor. In two minutes they were at the scene. The neighbor, a 70-year-old woman and another woman were the only persons on the street. Nobody else came forward. The man explained that he had called the police after much deliberation. He had phoned a friend for advice and then crossed the roof of the building to the apartment of the elderly woman to get her to make the call. 'I didn't want to get involved,' he sheepishly told the police.

Martin Gansberg, *New York Times*, 27 March 1964.

The OCR GCSE History A (SHP) course

The tables below show how 'Crime and Punishment' and 'Developments in Crime and Punishment, 1200–1945' are part of your history course. Your teacher will have chosen which topics your class are going to study.

FULL COURSE

Unit A951 (Study in Development and Study in Depth)	
Study in Development: You will study *one* of the following:	
Medicine Through Time	Crime & Punishment Through Time
Depth Study: You will study *one* of the following:	
Elizabethan England	
Britain, 1815–51	
The American West, 1840–1895	
Germany, 1919–1945	

Unit A951 is worth 45 per cent of your final mark.

In the questions on the Study in Development, you will need to interpret and evaluate sources of evidence; demonstrate knowledge and understanding of the key individuals, events, developments and issues, and compare and explain the factors and processes involved in change and development over a long period of time.

In the questions on the Study in Depth, you will have to demonstrate your understanding of people and problems in the past through your study of the social, economic, political, cultural and religious aspects of a country over a short period of time. These questions will encourage an issues-based and investigative approach to the content.

Unit A952 (Historical Source Investigation)	
You will study *one* of the following:	
Developments in British Medicine, 1200–1945	Developments in Crime and Punishment in Britain, 1200–1945

Unit A952 is worth 30 per cent of your final mark. It tests your ability to analyse and evaluate sources of evidence, using your knowledge of the topic to put the sources into their historical context

Unit A953 (Controlled Assessment)
You will study *one* of the following:
History Around Us: the investigation of a historical site and its historical context.
Modern World Study: the investigation of a current issue or problem from world events in the context of the past.
This unit of the course is worth 25 per cent of your final mark.

COURSE OBJECTIVES

As well as knowing which topics you are going to study, it is important to understand what skills you will be developing and assessed on.

- **AO1** – the ability to **recall, select and communicate** your knowledge and understanding of the historical topics you have studied.

- **AO2** – the ability to **explain and analyse**:
  - a key concepts such as causation, consequence, change and significance
  - b key features and characteristics of the periods studied and the relationship between them.

- **AO3** – the ability to understand, analyse and evaluate:
  - a a range of sources as part of a historical enquiry
  - b how aspects of the past have been interpreted and represented in different ways as part of a historical enquiry.

1.1 Law and order: Four eras of trying to keep the peace

What are the main 'law and order' issues being talked about today? What concerns the public? Source A is an article about the introduction of identity (ID) cards. The government thinks that the scheme will make a real difference to law and order, but some **civil liberties** groups are not so sure. Read the source and see what you think.

SOURCE A

Blunkett unveils ID card proposals

All UK residents could be required to hold a card with details of their identity under a controversial scheme outlined to the House of Commons today by the home secretary, David Blunkett.

But Mr Blunkett claimed that there was no question of the 'entitlement card' being a compulsory ID card that individuals would be required to carry at all times.

The proposal will now go to an open six-month consultation with the public, with Mr Blunkett insisting the government was 'neutral' on the issue – despite it being a never-realised pet project of both Labour and Conservative governments for more than 20 years.

And he stressed to those who objected to the idea on libertarian grounds: 'There is nothing to fear from our own identity being properly acknowledged and recognised.

'There is everything to fear from wrongful identification, or the acquisition of our identity for fraudulent purposes.'

The scheme most likely to be adopted would involve existing credit card-style driver's licences and the recently announced passport cards doubling up as entitlement cards, with a separate card for people who are eligible for neither of these documents.

Mr Blunkett said he was personally 'enthusiastic' about entitlement cards, which would be the first ID card scheme in the UK since the abandonment of wartime identity documents in 1952.

They could help combat illegal immigration and illegal working, fraud and identity theft, while at the same time helping people apply for benefits and services to which they were entitled, he said.

Mr Blunkett, launching a consultation document on the desirability of such cards, said they could provide 'a simple, straightforward and verifiable way for establishing the right to work legally'.

The home secretary said such a card could be required for the purpose of gaining access to services as well as employment.

The shadow home secretary, Oliver Letwin, told MPs that if the government was proposing a strictly defined benefit entitlement card, Tories would strongly welcome such a measure.

Mr Letwin said Mr Blunkett's statement was full of 'obscurity and spin' and warned that the public were bound to be anxious that the government planned to use such cards for a wide variety of other purposes.

Both of the two nationalist parties in parliament are opposed to the plan.

Scottish National Party Westminster home affairs spokeswoman Annabelle Ewing MP said:

'The SNP are opposed to identity cards on civil liberties grounds, and fear that the introduction of a voluntary scheme would be the thin end of the wedge towards compulsion.'

Simon Thomas, Plaid Cymru MP for Ceredigion, warned that the government is at risk of wasting millions of pounds on an ID card scheme while under-investing in our public services.

He said: 'There is no evidence that ID cards or entitlement cards would reduce fraud or the risk of terrorism. The September 11 bombers worked within a framework of ID cards and simply overcame it through stealing people's identities and forgery. There is no evidence either that ID cards on the continent have reduced fraud there.'

Article on the proposed introduction of ID cards from the *Guardian*, 3 July 2002.

By the end of this chapter you will have developed a clear understanding of the way law enforcement developed in Britain and why it was not easy to convince the British people that the actions taken were needed. You will learn about early police constables and how they were gradually replaced by paid professionals after the work of the Fielding Brothers and Robert Peel in London.

The **BIG QUESTION** that you will need to think about as you work through the chapter is:

> ## Have law and order and law enforcement in Britain improved over the last four eras?

ACTIVITIES

1 On the right is a list of statements that have applied to law officers over the centuries. For each statement decide whether you think it refers to law-keepers before 1450 or to modern police officers.

Do any of these statements surprise you? Why is that?

2 Create a Venn diagram to compare and contrast the roles of an early constable with a modern police officer; for example an area where they are similar is that they both aim to stop criminals. Also, a key difference is that early policing was undertaken by the whole community (of men), but modern police officers are trained and do this as a career. Use the statements in the previous activity to help you.

Put out fires and help with public safety

Never work alone

Do not have to bring people to justice

A job done by women and men

Very few of them for the population

Collect and record evidence carefully

Unpaid and unpopular work

Mostly operate at night

Part of specialist units

VOICE YOUR OPINION!

What is the debate about ID cards? Create a talking heads diagram like the one below that shows the different viewpoints clearly.

Government minister

Civil liberties group

1.2 Did Roman law progress in the 1000 years between Appius and Justinian?

LEARNING OBJECTIVES

In this lesson you will:
- learn about how the Romans dealt with law and order
- practise writing answers to change and continuity questions.

GETTING STARTED

What do you know about the Roman Empire? In groups of four, take a blank piece of paper and write 'Roman Empire' in the middle. Each take a side of the paper and for five minutes, silently, put down any ideas that come into your head. Share your ideas with the other three members of the group and agree on three statements that best sum up your work. Share these with the rest of the class.

In its early years Rome was a small **city-state** and the upper classes in society controlled law and order through an Assembly. As the empire grew there was a need to write down and make clear what the law was and whom it might affect.

In this lesson you will read the stories of two men who were involved in making and upholding Roman law – Appius Claudius and Emperor Justinian.

The first story is from the beginning of the empire and the second is from near the end. This will allow you to investigate whether law improved as time went on.

Fact file

Roman law enforcement – the structure of policing from 6 CE onwards

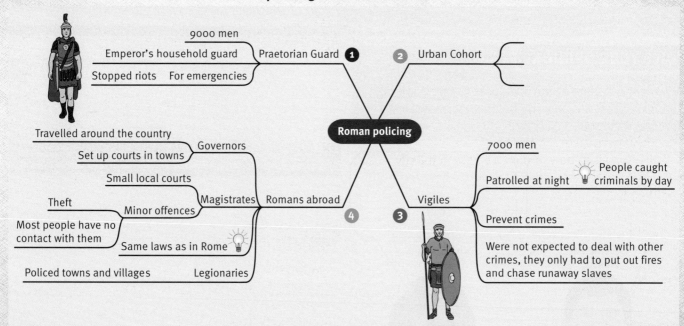

- Emperor's household guard — 9000 men
- Stopped riots — For emergencies
- Praetorian Guard **1**
- **2** Urban Cohort
- Travelled around the country
- Set up courts in towns — Governors
- Small local courts
- Theft — Minor offences — Magistrates — Romans abroad **4**
- Most people have no contact with them
- Same laws as in Rome
- Policed towns and villages — Legionaries
- Roman policing
- **3** Vigiles
- 7000 men
- Patrolled at night — People caught criminals by day
- Prevent crimes
- Were not expected to deal with other crimes, they only had to put out fires and chase runaway slaves

The Urban Cohorts consisted of about 3000 soldiers. They were not often seen on the streets of Rome, as it was not their job to patrol the streets. Their main duty was to stop riots. Riots were a frequent occurrence. The Urban Cohorts were used to keep order within the city, whereas the Praetorian Guard was there to protect the rulers of Rome.

1 As you read, note down some positives and negatives from each story on pages 5–6. Divide a sheet of paper into four and title it 'Roman Law'. Use the following headings: Positives – Appius Claudius; Positives – Emperor Justinian; Negatives – Appius Claudius; Negatives – Emperor Justinian. The positives should show that the law was progressing and making Rome a safer place to be. The negatives should be examples of how the law was unfair or put in danger by the actions of those in charge.

2 Look at the diagram of Roman law enforcement. Copy the diagram and complete the branch for Urban Cohorts.

3 Highlight similar information in each of the branches, for example, number of soldiers.

SOURCE A

Table I – If anyone summons a man before the magistrate, he must go. If the man summoned does not go, let the one summoning him call the bystanders to witness and then take him by force.

Table III – One who has confessed a debt, or against whom judgment has been pronounced, shall have thirty days to pay it in. After that, forcible seizure of his person is allowed.

Table IV – A dreadfully deformed child shall be quickly killed.

Table VII – Let them keep the road in order. If they have not paved it, a man may drive his team where he likes.

Table VIII – If one is slain while committing theft by night, he is rightly slain.

Table IX – Putting to death of any man, whosoever he might be, unconvicted, is forbidden.

Table X – None is to bury or burn a corpse in the city.

Table XI – Marriages should not take place between **plebeians** and **patricians**.

Table XII – If a slave shall have committed theft or done damage with his master's knowledge, the action for damages is in the slave's name.

Some of the laws of the Twelve Tables.

VOICE YOUR OPINION!

For each of the laws in Source A, decide whether any of them are still an issue today and which are completely out of date.

APPIUS CLAUDIUS, 451 BCE

In 451 BCE the Plebeian Council appointed a committee of 10 people – the Decemviri – to record the laws and make sure that everyone was clear about how to behave in public, private and politics. One of the 10 was Appius Claudius. The laws they set down became known as the Twelve Tables and were to be carved in copper and put on permanent display. Every schoolboy had to learn them and chant them in class. Source A shows some of the laws.

Rome now had a set of laws that everyone had to follow. They were public and so were trials. Everyone was treated fairly and had a right to be tried by their equals and to appeal against a sentence.

In theory, law and order should have been stable and things should have improved in the empire. Appius later met Virginia, the young daughter of a **centurian**. She resisted all his advances and so he got one of his supporters to pretend she was a slave and take her away. The centurian took the matter to Court, but when the trial started it was announced that Appius would be the judge. He, obviously, found in favour of his supporter and ordered that the girl become a slave. The centurian returned home and stabbed his daughter with a sword saying that he would prefer to see her die than be dishonoured.

The **Tribune** now became involved and they arrested Appius. While in custody he committed suicide.

ACTIVITIES

4 What does the list of laws in Source A tell you about Rome? Pick out the two that you think are the most revealing about life in Roman times and add them to your notes. Try to explain why they are significant.

5 Does your answer to question 4 match the ideas you had about Rome before starting this chapter? Why?

KEY WORDS

Centurian – an officer in the Roman Army.

City-state – an area that is controlled and governed entirely from one city.

Patricians – aristocracy.

Plebeians – ordinary people (people not belonging to the ruling class, no matter how much money they had).

Tribune – people's court.

Justinian (Emperor 527–65 CE)

Emperor Justinian was the son of a peasant, but was appointed Emperor by his uncle, who had risen through the ranks of the army to become ruler of Rome. Justinian was well educated and when he took control of Rome he set himself five aims. These were to:

1 stamp out corruption

2 refine and uphold the law

3 unite the Churches in the east

4 bring Christianity by force to the Barbarians in the west

5 recover Rome's lost territories.

In order to achieve the second aim, he established the Justinian Code in 529 CE. He collected together all the valid laws from across the empire. He also updated all the works of great thinkers on law. By 533 CE he had written a textbook on Roman law. In this way he planned to make sure that everyone was clear about what was acceptable behaviour. He ruled for a further 32 years.

'What have the Romans ever done for us?'

By the time Emperor Constantius Chlorus died in York in 306 on an expedition against the Picts [Scots], cities had sprung up around the original Roman forts linked to each other by a network of roads. Villas, baths, theatres, temples and administrative buildings were built... Britain's economy had developed rapidly through increased trade with the rest of the empire. Gravestones recorded the deaths of soldiers and civil servants from all over the Roman world, as well as those of the British who now took on Latin approximations of their names. The standard classical education turned them into scholars, administrators and orators...

M. Duffy, *England: The Making of the Myth*, 2001.

GradeStudio

You have just looked at the start of law and order and should now have a good understanding of how Rome tried to keep the peace. You have also been practising a key skill needed to achieve at GCSE: change and continuity. This exercise will help you to plan out and write a top-level answer for the following exam question:

c How far did Roman law and order change between 451 BCE (the beginning) and 565 CE (the end of the empire)? **[5 marks]**

Examiner's tip

Change and continuity questions usually begin with: 'How far did [the system of law and order] change between… ?'

It is important to recognise the key skills involved. You will need to have some changes and some continuity to talk about – the question says 'How far… ' so the examiner will want to see that you can make a judgement about what changed and what did not.

Below is a table to help you structure your first change and continuity question. Use the guidance in all three columns to help you build your answer. Once you have looked carefully, try to write an answer of your own.

What should I write about?	My answer	Structure and tips
PARAGRAPH 1 Change in Rome The *Decemviri* The Twelve Tables Justinian law	For example, '*The* Decemviri *were appointed to record the laws and make sure that everyone was clear about how to behave in public, private and politics. This would mean…* '	Write about each of the points and explain how they changed law and order in Rome At the end of the paragraph, create a mini-conclusion by referring back to the question.
PARAGRAPH 2 Continuity in Rome Corruption Policing Power with individuals	For example, '*The* Decemviri *became corrupt, especially Appius Claudius… Justinian was only appointed because his uncle was Emperor and not because he had a good understanding of the law*'	Write about each of the points and explain how they brought continuity to law and order At the end of the paragraph, create a mini-conclusion by referring back to the question.
CONCLUSION Judgement Supporting evidence Key point?	For example, '*Law and Order did not improve that much because policing methods were the same from 6 CE onwards. The Praetorian Guard and Urban Cohorts were only used on specific occasions like when there was a riot. In everyday life ordinary people had to catch criminals and bring them to court. Justinian changed the laws, but did not do anything to help prevent crime*'	Try to make a judgement: how much had changed? Was there more that changed or more that stayed the same? Can you explain why this is? Are there any reasons for this that are more important than the others? Why?

1.3 Case study: The Romans in Britain – What was unique about the Roman Empire?

LEARNING OBJECTIVES

In this lesson you will:

- learn about how the Romans dealt with law and order in Britain
- find evidence to make a case for significant change.

KEY WORDS

Client kings – *local leaders who retained power after invasion.*

Colony – *walled area of land controlled by military veterans from Rome.*

Governor – *Roman appointment in charge of a conquered area.*

Legion – *division of the Roman Army.*

Magistrate – *legal assistant to the Governor.*

GETTING STARTED

'In reaffirming the greatness of our nation, we understand that greatness is never a given. It must be earned. Our journey has never been one of shortcuts or settling for less.

It has not been the path for the faint-hearted, for those who prefer leisure over work, or seek only the pleasures of riches and fame.

Rather, it has been the risk-takers, the doers, the makers of things – some celebrated, but more often men and women obscure in their labor – who have carried us up the long, rugged path towards prosperity and freedom.

Barack Obama's Inauguration as President, 2009.

For us, they packed up their few worldly possessions and traveled across oceans in search of a new life. For us, they toiled in sweatshops and settled the West, endured the lash of the whip and plowed the hard earth.'

The event above has been described as one of the most significant in modern History. Why was Obama's election as President so significant?

ACTIVITY

1 As you read the information on this page, try to find evidence to support each of the 5Rs and decide whether the Romans brought significant change to law and order in Britain.

One way to judge whether events in the past were significant is to set criteria and test them out against evidence. Below are the 5Rs of significance in History – one method of looking at historical events.

1 **Revealing** – does it tell you a lot about the time?

2 **Results** – did it have a big effect on history?

3 **Remarkable** – did people talk about it?

4 **Remembered** – do people still mention it today?

5 **Relevant** – is it still important for us today?

These criteria should help you to judge whether the Romans coming to Britain was significant for law and order. We will consider the extent to which Roman Law was extended to the Empire and examine how subject nations were treated by the Romans.

Rome invaded Britain in two stages. The first was led by Julius Caesar, fresh from his conquest of Gaul (France). He attacked in 55 BCE, but achieved little. He returned the following year with a great army of five legions and in the Essex area installed a local ruler who was loyal to Rome. He was disappointed by lack of treasure though and did not return.

During the reign of Emperor Claudius, the family installed by Rome to govern Britain was ousted by a man called Caratacus. So, in 43 CE, Claudius sent a young general called Vespasian and four **legions** to invade Britain. The Britons were quickly defeated and it took only 30 years for the Romans to establish control over most of the country.

Organising law and order in Britain

There were two main figures of law and order in Roman Britain: the **Governor** and the **Magistrate**. Both were appointed by Rome and played a vital role in organising Law and Order.

SOURCE C

*Governors had to deal with **client kings** and keep them happy. They were also the main court of appeal in Britain and had to travel the country and sit as judge in local courts. If cases were serious and carried the death penalty, it was the role of the Governor to pass on information to the Emperor if a citizen appealed against a guilty verdict. It was the Governor though that had the final say in sentences for non-citizens.*
Anyone could be a Roman citizen. It was not based around blood or being born in Rome, it was about loyalty to the Roman ideals and service to the Empire. Many Britons assisted the Romans in their government and became citizens. This citizenship gave them a common identity with the rest of the Empire, but did not mean that law and government in their province changes. The Romans relied on local people and their customs – unless seen as outrageous – to help govern a conquered land.

Extract from Sheppard, Sunderland and Frere, *A History of Roman Britain*, 1987.

SOURCE D

The total number of Roman officials, at least in the civil part of the province, was not... unduly large. This was made possible by the encouragement of local self-government and responsibility among the conquered people.

Extract from Sheppard, Sunderland and Frere, *A History of Roman Britain*, 1987.

SOURCE B

A Roman vase found in Colchester. The scene depicts four gladiators.

Fact file

As they established control, the Romans set up three types of settlement. The first was a **'colony'**. These were urban areas controlled by Roman veterans and governed themselves under Roman Law. The second type of settlement was the 'municipium'. They were based around pre-existing towns. The third type was 'civitates pereginae'. They were large areas of rural land controlled by the Celts from country houses. The Romans were keen to involve conquered people in the running of their territory.

ACTIVITY

2 Create a counter argument. So far you have tried to find evidence for and prove that Roman changes in Britain were significant. Now, try to find evidence to support the opposite case, that changes were not significant. You might want to focus on the role of local people and local customs. Remember to think about the extent to which Roman law was extended to the Empire and how subject nations were treated by the Romans.

1.4 Have law and order improved?

Now that you have read about law and order in Roman times, you will need to begin thinking about the big question that we asked at the start of this chapter:

> ## Have law and order and policing in Britain improved over the last four eras?

In the next few lessons, you will find information about law and order from Saxon times to the present day. Your task is to look at the development of law and decide if there were any times when the state of law and order was worse than it is today. This will help you to reach a conclusion about that big question.

BRAIN BOOST

1 In Britain, from the Middle Ages to today, how effectively have people living in each era kept law and order? Read the main points for each time period in the chart, looking at:
   - **WHAT** happened
   - **WHO** were the key individuals
   - the **1 TO WATCH** sections, which highlight people or events that are crucial to understanding the development of law and order over time
   - the reasons WHY these events occurred.

   When you have finished, give each era a mark out of 10 for how effectively they kept law and order (10 would be a perfect society and 1 would be utter chaos). This is just an initial impression – as you work through the chapter, you will be able to come to a judgement on each era.

2 On your own copy of the table below create a hypothesis about law and order in Britain by highlighting the comments that show any improvement in policing and the law. Now, in a different colour, highlight all the comments that you think show little or no improvement. On balance, do you think that law and order has made much progress?

   As you go through the chapter, it will be important to add to your chart and fill in extra information. The most important section is the 'VERDICT' column. Once you have looked at an era, record how much protection you feel was given to people by scoring the progress made out of 10.

Time period	What?	Who?	Why?	Verdict
BRITAIN IN THE MIDDLE AGES 400–1485	Saxon law develops Hue and cry; Tithings Trial by ordeal Norman Conquest Constables **1 to Watch: Trial by ordeal**	King Alfred William of Normandy **1 to Watch: William**	Growth of religion War Trade Individuals **1 to Watch: Trade**	Three different ruling groups and lots of new laws... confusing? ?/10
EARLY MODERN BRITAIN 1485–1750	Constables, watchmen and justices of the peace (JPs) Travelling judges Wars of the Roses **1 to Watch: Constables**	Henry VII Jonathan Wild **1 to Watch: Henry VII**	War **1 to Watch: War**	Political stability by the end of the period but religious chaos... were thief-takers any good? ?/10
INDUSTRIAL BRITAIN 1750–1900	Growth of towns and cities The first paid constables Opposition to police **1 to Watch: Growth of towns**	The Fielding brothers Robert Peel **1 to Watch: Robert Peel**	War Taxation Social change Economic change **1 to Watch: Social change**	Napoleonic Wars and Peel's Police force... a popular move? ?/10
MODERN BRITAIN 1900–2000	More police Specialist units Racism Female police officers Transportation **1 to Watch: Specialist units**	The striking miners Stephen Lawrence **1 to Watch: Stephen Lawrence**	Social change Technology **1 to Watch: Technology**	Bad press for the police and specialist units... technological dream? ?/10

Four eras of law and order in Britain.

1.5 Was the age of the Saxons an uncivilised brawl?

LEARNING OBJECTIVES

In this lesson you will:

- learn about Saxon lawmakers and laws
- understand why events happen and that there can be several linked causes to explain a historical event.

The popular belief is that the Saxons were a lawless people, whose society was based around warriors and war. Source B, written around 20 years after the first Saxon raids on the south-east coast of England, tends to agree.

Fact file

'The Saxons' is a general term that covers many different groups of people who came from northern Europe. They were great warriors, but were also looking for new lands to settle in, where they could farm.

KEY WORDS

Ealdorman – *powerful local leader.*

Gemot – *people's court.*

Private courts – *run by local leaders to deal with minor crimes.*

Shire courts – *held in each county twice a year to deal with serious crimes.*

Wergeld – *compensation paid to victims after injury at the hands of another.*

Witan – *this was similar to our Houses of Parliament, where leading figures gathered to give advice on how the country should be run.*

GETTING STARTED

Look at Source A, a film poster about a legendary warrior called Beowulf whose adventures and customs had many similarities with the Saxons. What does the source suggest about Saxon life and Saxon leadership?

In pairs, come up with three words to describe:

a Saxon life

b Saxon leaders

Try to guess the plot of the film by analysing the poster. Write a synopsis of the story.

SOURCE

I am ripper, tearer, slasher. I am the teeth in the darkness. Mine is strength and lust and power. I am Beowulf!

Poster for the film *Beowulf*, 2007.

TIMELINE

Gildas the Monk writes about the arrival of Saxons

| 300 | 400 | 500 | 600 | 700 |

Britons appeal to Rome for military help

Aethelbert, first Christian king dies

They outdo all others in brutality. Ungovernable, entirely at home at sea, they attack unexpectedly. When they are ready to sail home they drown or crucify one in ten of their victims as a sacrifice, 'distributing the iniquity of death by the equity of lot'.

Sidonius Appollinaris, landowner, poet and later bishop, writing about Saxon raiders, c.470 CE.

This was a time of turmoil for Britain. From the departure of the Romans in around 410 CE the island became a rich prize for other nations and was raided or invaded several times. As tribes came in and settled, they brought with them new customs and ways of keeping law and order. Many Roman practices were lost or purposely destroyed.

The main change was that England was no longer governed by a single system but became a collection of smaller kingdoms, each with their own laws and customs. The timeline below helps to show what was happening.

The king had many responsibilities, including defending the kingdom and making sure the laws were obeyed. Kings did consult with the leading nobles and bishops (at the **Witan**) before making key decisions about law (see Source C). As laws started to be written, kings needed the help of monks to produce the documents. Most of these laws were about stopping violence and protecting the property of rich landowners.

Who played a part in making the law?

The role of the king got stronger as the Saxon period progressed, but there were also other groups involved in deciding and writing the law, including:

- nobles
- bishops
- monks.

The main Saxon law-makers.

The king	The nobles	The bishops	The monks

The king was the main law-maker and laws were issued in his name. He had responsibility over the entire kingdom and its safety. He had to make sure that the nobles were looked after and that violence was reduced. He also held the Witan meetings.	The nobles controlled the kingdoms of England and had complete authority within them. They were given this land by the king in return for their cooperation and assistance in times of war. They held their own **shire courts** and **private courts**.	The bishops controlled the Church and it was in the churches that people were taught about what was right and wrong through sermons. Bishops were also big landowners and needed protection. They were members of the Witan and helped to create the laws too.	Monks were under the control of the Church and took their orders from bishops. As Saxon law became more sophisticated it needed to be written down and this was the role of the monks. They were one of the few groups who could create documents.

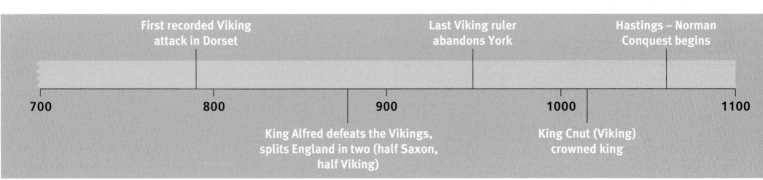

First recorded Viking attack in Dorset — 800

King Alfred defeats the Vikings, splits England in two (half Saxon, half Viking) — ~900

Last Viking ruler abandons York

King Cnut (Viking) crowned king — ~1000

Hastings – Norman Conquest begins

700 — 800 — 900 — 1000 — 1100

The Saxon laws

Below are examples of laws by three Saxon kings. Each was trying to address the problems that concerned him. Read them carefully and then answer the questions.

40. If an ear is struck off, 12 shillings shall be paid as compensation.

42. If an ear is lacerated, 6 shillings shall be paid...

The laws of Ethelbert, c.603.

SOURCE D

4. If any one plot against the king's life, of himself, or by harbouring of exiles, or of his men; let him be liable with his life and in all that he has...

6. If any one thieve caught in a church, let him pay the usual fine... and let the hand be struck off with which he did it.

19. If any one lend his weapon to another that he may kill some one therewith, they may join together if they will in the **wergeld**.

38. If a man fight before a king's **ealdorman** in the **gemot**, let him make with wergeld as it may be right; and before this 120 shillings to the ealdorman as a fine.

The laws of King Alfred, 871–899.

SOURCE E

12. But if it be found that any of these have given wrongful witness, that his witness never stand again for aught, and that he also give thirty shillings as a fine.

The laws of Athelstan, 924–39.

VOICE YOUR OPINION!

How far can invasion and war be a cause of change?

Think about the reaction of some Iraqi people to the presence of British and US troops in their country. Is this helping to create change? Has the war made any difference to Iraq? Is it in a better position than before the conflict?

Now, think about how a Saxon takeover would have affected Britain.

SOURCE F

A Saxon king and his advisers at the Witan (royal court).

ACTIVITIES

1 Look at Source B. Why might raiders of a country be viewed in this way?

2 Look at the timeline on pages 11–12. Choose an image for each event, then rank order them with the one that you think would have had the biggest impact on law and order at the top. Give reasons for your choices.

3 Using the information in the table on the main Saxon lawmakers and from the first part of this lesson, complete the link diagram below. Simply draw a line between two boxes that link and write the connection along the line – there is an example to help you. Find as many links as you can.

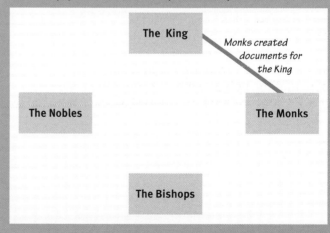

4 What issues caused the kings to make new laws? What does this tell you about Saxon times and the problems faced by the king?

5 Do you think that making laws was enough to stop people committing crimes? What else would be needed?

1.6 Was trial by ordeal a barbaric and irrational way of finding guilt?

LEARNING OBJECTIVES

In this lesson you will:

- learn about the Saxon courts, trial by jury and trial by ordeal
- select evidence based on how much it reveals about the Saxons.

GETTING STARTED

Who am I? (Guess the character from an earlier lesson.)

- I was ruler for 28 years.
- I divided England.
- I devised a detailed code of law.

Saxon courts and trial by jury

From 600 CE the Saxon kingdoms of England vied for power between themselves with each kingdom having its own set of laws, such as the laws of Offa of Mercia and the laws of Aethelbert of Kent. Then throughout the 9th century Viking attacks on Britain became more frequent and larger areas were conquered, settled and ruled by Scandinavians. They brought with them their own laws and traditions, and the areas they ruled became known as the Danelaw.

Type of court	Information
Witan	Attended by the king and the leading nobles and bishops. It made laws and dealt with very serious cases, and also crimes involving the nobles.
Shire court	England was divided into shires and each one had its own 'shire-reeve' (sheriff). He normally organised trials, with other landowners present. The shire court met twice a year for serious cases.
Hundred court	Each shire was divided into 'hundreds' (areas containing roughly 100 peasant farms). The court had to be attended by all **freemen** and met monthly to deal with minor cases and set up tithings.
Burgh court and private court	Towns that had received a **royal charter** also had burgh courts. There were private courts held by landowners in their villages. These dealt with work issues and the cases involving slaves.

The system of courts in England by 1000.

After King Alfred the Great of Wessex divided England with the Danes in 886, the Saxons did not close off all communication with them. They took some of their ideas and used them. For example, the 12-person jury, still used today, was a Danish practice adopted by the Saxons.

Alfred also produced his own code of laws that brought together laws from the various Saxon kingdoms and had them written into a law book. He chose to use those laws that he considered 'most just'.

ACTIVITIES

1. Why do you think there were so many different courts?
2. What were the Saxons trying to achieve?

KEY WORDS

Freemen – *people who were not slaves or peasants. They did not have to work on the lord's land and were not controlled by him.*

Royal charter – *allowed towns to appoint their own officials and govern themselves.*

Trial by ordeal – *deciding whether someone was guilty by using tests that involved pain. It was used if the accused was a suspicious character, had often been accused of crimes or if the jury could not reach a decision.*

Map of England, 886 CE.

Fact file

Trial by jury was an important part of the legal system. Cases would be heard with the victim and the accused each presenting their own case. The jury – usually made up of local villagers who would know both people – would have to decide who was telling the truth. The accused could bring in 'compugators' to talk about their good character. They had to swear an oath first; juries did listen to their evidence, especially if they were important people.

ACTIVITY

3   Imagine that you are making a TV documentary about **trial by ordeal**. You have watched hours of footage from other history programmes and they all show the practice as brutal and sadistic. However, they do not show the context behind the events or attempt to explain why the Saxons used these methods.

Look at the information given about each part of the programme below and the footage available to you. Then decide which shots to use and in what order. Give each scene a title. You can only use a maximum of two shots per scene and you need to explain your choices.

Information for the narration	Choice of footage		
Scene 1 Trial by ordeal could only be used after all other avenues when the court decided that the best way to progress was to hand the matter over to God. They had absolute faith that God would deliver the correct judgement. These public trials were controlled by the Church.	Crowd gathering to watch a trial by ordeal. They look like they enjoy it	Priest being visited by a shire-reeve	Saxon jury looking puzzled and conferring
Scene 2 Preparation was very thorough. The person involved had to fast for three days before the trial and hear mass in the local church. Most of the trials took place in the church.	Priest delivering a sermon in church and people praying	Man refusing food and sitting with his eyes closed	Local people staring at the accused and pointing
Scene 3 Trial by hot iron was mostly taken by women. The accused must walk three paces holding a bar of red hot metal. The wounds were then wrapped for three days. If they healed then God was showing they were innocent of the crime. An infected wound was a sign of guilt.	Woman carrying the hot bar	Man carrying the hot bar with look of pain on his face	Hands with bandages being taken off
Scene 4 The accused had to pick up an object such as a ring from the bottom of a cauldron of boiling water blessed by the priest. Their hand was bandaged for three days, and if the wound was clean then the person was innocent. This ordeal was mostly used on men.	Man with hand in cauldron – laughing crowd behind	Shot of cauldron being set up by priest outside	Man with hand in cauldron – serious crowd behind
Scene 5 The accused was lowered into a river or pond as people believed that water was pure and would reject anyone who was not pure themselves. The innocent would therefore sink and the guilty float. This was normally used for slaves, but could be for anybody.	Crowd turning their backs in horror	Shot of village green with duck pond and normal life	Close up of accused in absolute terror
Scene 6 A trial by ordeal for a priest involved him eating consecrated (holy) bread. If he choked on it he was guilty because God would not allow a sinner to eat consecrated bread. If he ate it normally then he was innocent.	Picture of the holy sacrament	Priest praying	Priest looking relaxed and eating

1.7 How much did Saxon law and order progress?

LEARNING OBJECTIVES

In this lesson you will:

- examine the level of progress that occurred in law and order during the Saxon period
- improve your analysis and evaluation skills by carefully considering a range of evidence.

ACTIVITIES

1 Firstly, create your own version of the cards and then sort them into three columns: **law and order; crime; punishment**.

2 Next, place the cards on a continuum that goes from **no progress** to **great progress**. In what area was there most progress? How can you explain this?

3 Look at Source A. Create a plaque to fit on the front of the statue's plinth that gives a short summary of the difference King Alfred made to crime and punishment in the Saxon era.

In the previous sections you have examined Saxon laws and have seen how the Saxons tried to keep order. There were many changes that took place during the Saxon period, but were they all for the good? Below are a set of cards that summarise Saxon crime and punishment.

The *wergeld* for killing a noble was 1200 shillings.	The King was the main law maker, but the nobles controlled the kingdoms.	Tithings were responsible for capturing cattle rustlers and families for getting thieves.
The Church is where people learned right and wrong.	Anglo-Saxon rulers were most worried about treason, violence and theft in society.	The death penalty was used for serious crimes like treason, murder and housebreaking.
Many runaway slaves became dangerous bandits and robbers, or joined the Vikings.	Monks started to write down important laws so that they could be referred to.	Edmund decreed that runaway slaves had to be rounded up by the tithings (959).
In 901 Wulfhere lost his lands for deserting the King.	The spread of Christianity helped to end the practice of the Blood Feud.	King Alfred (871–99) created a comprehensive set of laws to help govern his lands.
Local leaders were able to adapt punishments to suit their local customs.	The Witan was a meeting of leading bishops and nobles who advised the King.	Aethelstan (924–39) relaxes the law regarding the monitoring of trade.

SOURCE A

A statue of King Alfred in his old capital of Winchester.

Why was John Scot beheaded?

The year is now 1281, 200 years after the last Anglo-Saxon king ruled England. A travelling court presided over by a judge (eyre) has arrived in Derbyshire and the following case has been presented (see Source B).

SOURCE B

John Scot lodged at the house of John Wenge in Ekynton, rose by night wishing to do away with John Wenge, who seeing this, raised the hue.

John Scot fled at once. Richard, former groom of Hugh de Cantilupo, hearing the hue, joined in and together they pursued John Scot whom they beheaded as a thief in flight.

1281 Derbyshire Eyre, Case 454, National Archives.

ACTIVITY

You must now take on the role of an investigator for the court.

4 Use Source B and the information about the medieval justice system below to determine whether anyone should be punished for the death of John Scot.

The hue was a gathering of local people who chased the suspected criminal.	Everyone who heard the cry had to join the hue, or face a heavy fine.
There was no police force; people had to rely on friends and families.	Local communities had a strong sense of justice and dealt with crime harshly.
The 'hue and cry' had to be called if a crime had been committed.	An attempted crime could be punished by using that act on the criminal.
All males over the age of 12 had to belong to tithings.	The victim of a crime had to cry out the name of the crime for others to hear.
If one of the 10 men in a tithing committed a crime, then the others had to bring him to justice.	The king needed local people to organise law and order.

BRAIN BOOST

You have just completed a thinking skills activity that completes the section on the Saxons. Now is a good time to help your brain remember what you have learned…

STEP ONE – Pick out what you think are the four key ideas from this section on Saxons and write a short paragraph about each one.

STEP TWO – Summarise each paragraph by giving it a heading and highlighting four key words.

STEP THREE – Pick out the one word that is most important in each paragraph and create an image to go with each one (turning text into images helps the brain make connections).

STEP FOUR – Create a story in your mind that involves the four key words and images.

VOICE YOUR OPINION!

Does this mean that the John Scot case proves that policing had not changed between the Saxon and medieval periods?

In the last lessons you have been examining Saxon law. However, John Scot's death occurred in 1281, during the medieval period. In 1066, the Normans conquered England and brought their own system of government and laws. Yet both tithings and the hue and cry were a vital part of Saxon policing.

1.8 What happened to law and order after the Norman Conquest?

LEARNING OBJECTIVES

In this lesson you will:
- learn about how the Normans changed law and order
- analyse a source and make several points about it.

GETTING STARTED

Imagine that you have been put in charge of your school. Make a list of five changes you would make to the way the school is run or organised.

Now next to each point add a sentence saying what sort of things you would need to make sure this change happened.

The Norman Conquest

The Norman Conquest began when King Edward (the Confessor) died in 1066 and three people challenged for the throne. They were King Harald Hardrada of Norway, Duke William of Normandy and Earl Harold Godwineson of Wessex, who was actually crowned king. William of Normandy believed that he had been promised the throne by Edward the Confessor and so he invaded in October. He defeated Harold Godwineson at the Battle of Hastings who himself had already defeated Harald Hardrada at the Battle of Stamford Bridge. William entered London victorious and was crowned King of England on Christmas Day 1066.

The triumph of William the Conqueror brought a new system to England. Although England had always had a feudal system with landowners and lords, the Normans made it more rigid and needed to show that they were the ones in charge. It put villeins (peasants) firmly at the bottom.

With only between 5000 and 8000 Norman knights to help rule the country the Normans needed to enforce law and order strictly to stay in power. They brought the shire reeves (or sheriffs), who had been largely left to run each county in their own way, under central control.

The Norman feudal system

King

Provides money and knights

Grants land to

Barons

Provide protection and military service

Grants land to

Knights

Provide food and services when demanded

Grants land to

Villeins

The Norman feudal system.

GradeStudio

Examiner's tips

In the exam, you can get the top marks for looking at more than one reason, so try to group the boxes or some of their content to create several reasons why people felt law and order needed to be addressed.

Fact file

Thomas Aquinas was a 13th-century philosopher and probably the first really important thinker in the British Isles. His ideas were concerned with what makes us act the way we do and how we live our lives.

1   How philosophical are you? Source A contains some of the thoughts of Thomas Aquinas, written between 1265 and 1274. First of all, analyse what Thomas Aquinas is trying to say about law and order. In your exercise book, explain what he means by each of the statements (there is an example for you to look at).

2   Why was Aquinas so concerned about law and order at this particular time? Look at the information boxes and assess how much impact each one would have had on people's views. Rank order these reasons to show which two you feel are most important. Try to find links between the different factors.

3   The Norman Conquest certainly changed England. List the four changes that you feel are the most important.

4   Go back to the chart you started in lesson 1.4 and add key events, key people and factors to the columns.

Heirs to Edward the Confessor
At first the Normans changed little, they wanted to show that they were the true heirs of 'the Confessor'. William did introduce the forest laws, making 30% of England royal forest, not to be used by others.

Trade
Trade had slowly been growing through Saxon times and now exploded. With so much trade and wealth around, leaders became worried that the pursuit of wealth was not compatible with the ideas of law and order.

Society can be perfect and laws should help to make it

SOURCE A

*... since each single man is a part of the **perfect community**, law necessarily concerns itself particularly with **communal happiness**.*

*Everyone knows the **truth** to some extent, since at least the **common principles** of natural law are available to him.*

*There is a certain aptitude for **virtue** in man, but the perfection of that virtue must be achieved through **training**... This is particularly true of the young, who are also more easily trained. Thus the training through which men come to virtue needs to be received from someone else.*

*Nevertheless, since some are not easily moved by words because they are **depraved** and **inclined to vice**, it is necessary for such to be restrained from evil by force and fear, so that they will at least stop their evil-doing and **leave others in peace**, or perhaps eventually, by force of habit, be brought to do willingly what they formerly did through fear, thus becoming virtuous. This kind of training, which compels through **fear of punishment**, is the training of laws.*

Thus it was necessary for peace and virtue that there be laws.

Extracts from *Summa theologiae* by Thomas Aquinas, written 1265–74.

Trial by battle
A new ordeal was introduced: trial by battle. The Normans believed that God would favour the innocent in battle. The guilty would either be killed or give in. If he did give in he would be hanged.

Change of language
With a change of language came new words. French and Latin words came into the English language like *gaol*, *police* and *justice*.

Land and ownership
William gave land to his followers, but in return he expected them to keep order. The role of the tithing and communities solving their own problems was slowly eroded by lords gaining more power.

1.9 Did the Islamic Empire or Medieval England have the strongest system of law and order in the Middle Ages?

LEARNING OBJECTIVES

In this lesson you will:

- learn about how Islamic and English law and order changed by 1450
- compare and contrast to reach conclusions.

ACTIVITY

1 Create a Venn diagram to compare and contrast Islamic and English Law in the Middle Ages. In particular you might want to look at the following:
   - Judges and Juries
   - The State and its role
   - Punishments
   - Religion
   - Debate and review of the law

Islamic law and order

In the Islamic Empire that was growing across the Middle East and Africa, life was governed by a set of religious laws based around the holy book, Qur'an. The five pillars of Islam were the main rules that people followed, but the most important aspects of life were covered by the law. The law had its own scholars and judges, and both these groups were among the most respected in Islamic society. They aimed to divide every act into one of five categories: compulsory, permitted, neutral, discouraged and forbidden. This body of law governed the lives of Muslims and formed the basis of law and order in the Islamic world.

Traditional Islamic law is called *Sharia*, an Arabic word meaning 'the right path'. Sharia is based on the Qur'an and the teachings of the Prophet Muhammad and interpretations of his words.

During the Middle Ages, Islamic law was split. The government dealt with criminal cases and the *kadis* handled cases involving religious, family, property, and commercial law.

The law was debated regularly and, as a consequence, regions of the Islamic Empire developed different practises and standards. However, written guidance was available to all judges on how to make the law work.

Sharia law allowed some rights for women which was unusual for the Middle Ages. They could obtain a decree to leave their husbands from *kadis* and

inherit land and wealth. Men still had the vast majority of rights and were legally responsible for the women they lived with (wives and daughters).

Some crimes appear in the Qur'an and were considered the most serious. These all had fixed punishments:

Offence	Punishment
Drinking alcohol	80 lashes
Slander	80 lashes
Theft	First offence – right hand cut off Second offence – left foot cut off Further offences – imprisonment
Highway robbery	Execution Crucifixion Exile Imprisonment Right hand and left foot cut off
Adultery	Stoned to death

In cases where people were killed or injured, the family of the victim had a right to retaliate. However, the law was that the retaliation had to be exact in proportion to the crime and if the damage done was more severe than the crime, the victim or his avenger could end up in prison. This discouraged people from taking part and so another system emerged. Here, people accepted payment instead – 'blood money'. The avenger therefore had a great responsiblilty. They had to bring the accused to court and then get the punishment right.

For smaller offences, the judges decided on the punishment.

Medieval law – Henry's reforms

The Medieval system of law and order seems harsh and severe, but it needed to be. Without a regular police force or independent system of catching criminals, the easiest way to ensure people stayed lawful was to scare them into it. Even petty crimes carried serious punishments.

As outlined on pages 14–15, people accused of crimes often had to go through one of three ordeals:

Ordeal by fire, Ordeal by water and Ordeal by battle.

Another, less common, ordeal was Ordeal by Bread. It was usually for the nobility, and worked by forcing the accused to eat a full slice of bread without chewing. If the accused choked, he was guilty. If he didn't choke, then he had God on his side and was innocent.

When Henry II came to the throne in 1154 he saw a system that had stopped working and was outdated. The baronial civil war that had plagued England for the previous nine years had ground the legal system to a halt. Therefore, restoring the peace and authority of the King was his most important task. This meant taking control of the barons and making sure that they knew he was in charge.

SOURCE A

Orford Castle, a sign of the power of Henry II.

An example of this in action can be seen in Suffolk. Hugh Bigod controlled large areas of land from his castle at Framlingham. He was disloyal to the King and so had had his lands confiscated. However, in 1165 he bought back Framlingham castle, but Henry had since had a Royal Castle built nearby at Orford, to remind Bigod of his authority.

Another problem was Church Law. The Church had its own set of rules and some were not compatible with English Law. The Church tried to get the law changed to match its own, but Henry and the barons resisted, saying 'we do not wish to change the laws of England'. English Law still had similarities with the French system the Normans had brought over, but it now had its own identity, separate from other nations and also from the Church. It was partly this idea that led to Henry II's famous dispute with Thomas Becket, where the Archbishop ended up being killed by the King's knights.

Royal legislation, known as assizes, was issued at Clarendon in 1166 and Northampton in 1176 in an effort to reduce serious crime. Royal justices were told by Henry to travel widely and deal with crime. In each location, the judges were assisted by twelve local men who made up a jury. Everyone who appeared in front of the jury was to be put to ordeal by water and if found guilty they would lose a foot or, after 1176, their right hand.

Henry also made changes to land law, especially dispossession and inheritance diputes. The King made sheriffs present information to a jury for a quick decision. This speedy approach and settlement proved popular and reduced the number of ordeals by battle. Henry's laws also protected tenants against their lords. The barons were exempt from this and it led to their protest under King John, the *Magna Carta*.

ACTIVITY

2 Do you remember the key question for this spread:

Did the Islamic Empire or Medieval England have the strongest system of law and order in the Middle Ages?

Think of five criteria that would make any system of law and order strong and list them. Test both the Islamic and English systems and see how many criteria they meet.

1.10 Why did Britons have to fight for their rights?

LEARNING OBJECTIVES

In this lesson you will:
- learn about the causes of protest in medieval England
- analyse patterns of history and identify turning points.

KEY WORDS

Civil Service – *people who carry out duties and administration for the Crown.*

Common law – *the system of law based on the decisions of the courts and old customs; still used in the legal system today.*

ACTIVITY

1 The picture shows a journey from 'Stable Common' to 'Tudor Mansion'. It takes in many of the major flash points from 1150–1485. Your task is to name each road appropriately and suggest road signs that could be put along the way. The first sign has been completed for you.

Henry III angered the barons by giving important roles in government to foreign nobles. As a protest, Simon de Montfort, leader of the opposition to the king, summoned town council leaders and knights to a meeting. This was the first time that commoners had met to discuss the way the country was ruled; it was known as a meeting of the 'commons'.

Henry II established **common law**, and a **Civil Service**. He also created his own private army by taxing the barons in cash, rather than making them supply troops for the army. In this way he was able to reduce the power of the barons, since they now had no need for their own armed men.

King John 1199–1216

Henry III 1216–72

King John fought many wars and argued with the Pope. The barons also disliked his rule and in 1215 forced him to sign Magna Carta to guarantee their rights.

A rebellion, led by Simon de Montfort, was easily crushed within a few months.

WORKFORCE
SLOW

Henry II 1154–89

Henry spent much of his time in France defending his territories. His son, Richard I, was also either in France or fighting in the Crusades. England continued to be ruled this way until the reign of King John (1199–1216).

Stable common

SOURCE Ⓐ

No freeman shall be arrested or imprisoned or dispossessed or outlawed or banished or in any way molested, nor will we go upon him nor send upon him, except by the lawful judgement of his peers and the law of the land.

Clause from Magna Carta, 1215.

Edward II governed badly and the barons decided to take control of England after murdering Edward's lover, Piers Gaveston. The Scots invaded England under Robert the Bruce and defeated an army led by the barons of England.

SOURCE B

At home the Hundred Years War had encouraged anarchy, litigation and lawlessness as the lords built up their private armies to go in search of plunder in France. When France was lost the mercenary bands came back to England to fight in the Wars of the Roses.

M. Duffy, *England* (a modern history book), 2001.

Edward II 1307–26

Edward and Parliament defeated the barons and took control again, however Edward's relationship with Hugh le Despenser upset his queen, Isabella, and so she plotted to dethrone him. Edward was eventually imprisoned and killed.

Edward III 1327–77

Edward III made a peace settlement with the Scots but in 1337 he began the Hundred Years War with France.

Henry IV had to deal with the growth of a religious group known as the Lollards. This movement wanted to create an English Church for the English people, not one controlled by the Pope. The movement was popular among the people and some of the gentry too, but the authorities were still nervous after the Peasants' Revolt and crushed the movement.

Richard II 1377–99

War with France caused huge problems and led to problems with crime. It also allowed the rise of over-mighty barons which led to the Wars of the Roses.

Henry IV 1399–1413

Richard II was only 10 years old when he came to the throne and so most of the decisions were being taken by advisers. An unpopular tax to pay for war in France led to the Peasants' Revolt in 1381. The rebels demanded freedom for the ordinary man and redistribution of wealth. King Richard met with them to discuss their demands, but it ended with the rebel leader being killed.

Tudor mansion

Wars of the Roses 1453–87

ACTIVITIES

2 What caused rebellions in medieval times? Make a list of all the things that sparked off conflict.

3 At what point on the road map do you feel the kings of England faced their biggest challenge? Why?

Richard III 1485–1509

A rebellion against King Richard III led to his defeat in battle, ending the Wars of the Roses. Henry VII came to the throne and brought a period of relative stability to England.

1.11 Get your sources sorted!

A case study for the early modern period. Did Henry VII revolutionise law and order or just do what was necessary to survive as king?

LEARNING OBJECTIVES

In this lesson you will:

- learn about law and order at the time of Henry VII
- practise answering questions that ask you to give your impression of a source or ask you to consider how useful a source is.

The cover of a bellman poem written in the 1600s.

Henry VII became king of England in 1485. This marks the end of the Middle Ages and the beginning of the early modern period.

When Henry VII became king of England, he was faced with a difficult task. He had just defeated Richard III in battle and so was not a legitimate heir to the throne. There was the possibility that he could face rebellions against him – after all, he had staged one to become king. He therefore needed to make sure that local leaders did not become too strong and that the people followed the law. He decided to cut most of the powerful noblemen out of the system (except his most trusted supporters) and to give power to lesser nobles. He also wanted to make sure that no one person was in charge of law and order within a county.

Impressions questions and utility questions

This exercise will help you to plan out and write a top-level answer for two different types of source-based exam question:

- questions where you are asked to give your impressions of a source
- questions where you are asked to consider how useful a source is – its utility.

How to answer a 'what impressions' question

> **a** Study Source A. What impressions of bellmen does the source give you? Use the source and your own knowledge to explain your answer.
>
> **[5 marks]**

Step one: Read the question, identify and highlight the following:

- the topic (bellmen)
- the time frame (none stated)
- the question type (what impressions).

Step two: Pick out information and say what it suggests (actually use the word *suggests*).

For example, 'The man has a vicious-looking dog and this suggests that the job was dangerous'.

Find three more examples.

Now move on and look at the more difficult question that follows.

How to answer a 'how useful' question

> **b** Study Source B. How useful is this source as evidence about the effectiveness of bellmen in the early modern period? Use the source and your knowledge to explain your answer.
>
> **[5 marks]**

Step one: Find some 'negative' points that show the source is not useful. Again, you could look at the content of the source or the attribute.

For example, 'However, this is fictional and so some of the information may be exaggerated'.

Find two more points.

Step two: Look at the viewpoint the source tries to portray and evaluate this. Every source has a viewpoint and if you can recognise this and still see positive and negative points then you will get top marks.

For example, 'The author has shown a very positive image of the bellman and is therefore supporting law and order efforts. Like songs, poems are written to be popular and this shows that people must have believed bellmen were needed and effective. It might not have been accurate in all cases, but shows what most people thought'.

ACTIVITIES

Below is a table containing information about the people who gained extra powers over law and order up to the time of Henry VII.

Your task is to answer the following question:
Were the changes in law and order made up to the reign of Henry VII an improvement on the tithings and 'hue and cry' system? Use the following steps to help build your answer.

1 Read about the people listed in the table and say how they helped to keep law and order in Britain.

2 Now, try to put law enforcement in a hierarchy. Show the law and order process for a country village and town using a chart.

3 Now, have a go at putting a whole answer together. If you are feeling brave choose a different source from another lesson.

Remember to add some more comments and key points to your chart from the beginning of the chapter.

Travelling Judge	The criminal cases that were too difficult or serious for JPs to deal with went to the assize courts. These were held in each county every six months. They were controlled by judges under special commission from the Crown, who travelled the country to make sure that cases were heard and justice done.
Justice of the Peace (JP)	JPs owed their offices to the king and took over from sheriffs as the chief local government officers. JPs were responsible for public order in their area and were responsible for enforcing the law. Most JPs were local landowners and so had a vested interest in protecting property and having good order in society. The average number of JPs per county was 18. The most senior JP in a county was usually a bishop. No JP was paid for his work.
Constable	Each county was divided into hundreds and each hundred or village had a constable. However, JPs found it difficult to find volunteers, because people were reluctant to be the 'face' of the law. Constables were usually the wealthier villagers who volunteered for a year. Everyone was supposed to take a turn, but many people paid others to do their duty for them.
Watchmen/ Bellman	Watchmen and bellmen had a similar job to constables, but were based in the towns. They had to walk the streets and call out the hour to reassure people that everything was as it should be. They worked at night, but some of the larger towns had day patrols too. Their job also involved alerting people when a crime had been committed.
Mayor	Mayors and aldermen were the equivalent of the JPs in the towns. They were usually well-respected businessmen and were appointed to uphold the law and keep order. They could give out punishments for minor crimes and had to deal with the 'problem' of vagrants (homeless people).
Thief-takers	With no centralised police force to help prevent and solve crimes until well into the 19th century people would often turn to private individuals who offered their services as thief-takers. They would be hired in the main by the victims of a crime or their family and their task would be to uncover those responsible for the crime. The majority of their work concerned theft and they would often negotiate for the return of the stolen property. There were numerous instances where the thief-taker was in league or even ran the gangs responsible for the crimes in the first place.

A summary of law enforcement in the late medieval period.

1.12 Have the historians got the right idea about law and order in the Early Modern Period?

LEARNING OBJECTIVES

In this lesson you will:

- explore the conclusions of historians about the period
- make a judgement how accurate claims are and whether there is evidence to back them up.

Historians like making conclusions and working out a theory about what happened in a particular era or event. Sometimes, this is vital because the book they are producing has to summarise lots of topics in a short space. You are going to test one of these pieces of writing and see if it holds up under scrutiny. The writer is John Guy, one of Britain's leading experts on Tudor and Stuart England. The extract comes from a popular book called *The Oxford History of Britain* which aims to summarise all of the nation's history. Source A below is what he said about law and order in the Early Modern Period:

SOURCE A

There was no police force at all. Few crimes were 'investigated' by the authorities. Criminal trials resulted from accusations and evidence brought by victims and aggrieved parties to the attention of the justices of the peace. Arrests were made by village constables, ordinary farmers or craftsmen taking their turn for a year, or by sheriffs (gentlemen also taking their turn) who did have a small paid staff of bailiffs. Riots and more widespread disorders could be dealt with by the militia or a 'posse comitatus', a gathering of freeholders specially recruited for the occasion by the sheriff.

Extract from John Guy's *The Oxford History of Britain.*

SOURCE B

The watchman, an old type of policeman found in many parts of the world, had, in England, an ancient legal basis in Edward I's statute of Winchester (1285). But he was not, strictly speaking, a police officer. That description is properly applicable only to the constable, who came into existence during the reign of Henry III.

From John Maylan, *The Police of Britain*, 1948.

ACTIVITIES

Historians need to be accurate, detailed and give a sense of the period they are analysing. You are going to assess John Guy's conclusion in Source A using these criteria and award him up to three stars for each category.

1 Think about and then write a definition for what a one star, two star and three star response might need to include.

2 Use the evidence from the sources to rate how successful John Guy's conclusion is. Use a table like the one below to help organise your work. Make sure you analyse each sentence in Source A.

Star rating	*	**	***
Definition			
Accuracy			
Detail			
Sense of period			

3 Sum up how well John Guy did with his conclusion.

A nightwatchman with his lantern, rattle and stick from 1750.

Inquisition held at Dartford 14 May 1595, before John Walker, coroner, on the body of James Lee of Dartford, yeoman. A jury found that Lee attacked Richard Hudson of Dartford with a sword (worth 20d). Fearing for his life, Hudson, in self-defence struck Lee with his sword (worth 12d) inflicting a wound from which he died on 10 May. Self-defence.

Record from Dartford assizes in the 16th century.

George Marwell of Dartford, labourer, indicted for grand larceny. On 1 May 1564 at Dartford he stole 5 sheep (worth 24s.6d) from William Vaughan. On 31 May at Dartford, he stole 5 sheep (worth 17 shillings) from William Vaughan. Not guilty.

Record from Dartford assizes in the 16th century.

A List of Proper persons to serve the Offices of Petty Constable and Headboroughs of the parish of Rotherhith for the year 1747

Petty Constable: James Frederick, Grocer

Headboroughs: Edmond Drayton, Upholsterer; John Walker, Brickemaker; John Woodjohn, Blacksmith; John Taylor, Dealer in Timber; Peter Thomas, Brewer; Samuel Forty, Baker

List of Law enforcers in Rotherhithe for 1747. Headboroughs were like petty constables, but had slightly less power.

Most of the sheriff's law enforcement duties, such as serving writs and making arrests, were carried out by his undersheriff and a team of bailiffs.

Bailiffs, like gaolers, were not hired for their charm and gentle manners; sheriff's officers were notorious for being corrupt and disorderly, often appearing in the archdeacon's court on charges of drunkenness.

Extract from Michael Best's 'Officers of the law: the arrest' in *Shakespeare's Life and Times*, 2001.

Prior to 1829 the military had often to be called upon in London and elsewhere, not merely to deal with riots or tumults but for ordinary work of patrolling the streets when small disorders were threatened…

Extract from Michael Best's 'Officers of the law: the arrest' in *Shakespeare's Life and Times*, 2001.

1.13 Was London really the 'apocalypse of evil'?

LEARNING OBJECTIVES

In this lesson you will:

- learn about the impact of the Industrial Revolution on London
- be able to demonstrate how these developments affected law and order.

GETTING STARTED

Using Sources A and B, as a class, create an ideas map like the one below by adding one or two ideas about England in the 1800s on sticky notes. Then add these to the board or any other suitable display area. Discuss your ideas.

KEY WORDS

Industrial Revolution – *when a country moves from an agricultural economy to one based on industrial methods of production. Britain was the first country to have an industrial revolution.*

SOURCE A

If a late twentieth-century person were suddenly to find himself in a tavern or house of the period, he would be literally sick – sick with the smells, sick with the food, sick with the atmosphere around him.

A description of Victorian London, from P. Ackroyd, *Dickens*, 1990.

Poverty

Dirty

What was England like in the 1800s?

Industry

SOURCE B

The Haunted Lady, or the Ghost in the Looking Glass.

Why did life change in Britain?

The period 1750–1900 witnessed a major shake-up and change in both the economy and society of Britain. It was known as the **Industrial Revolution**. It transformed society down to its very roots. Like the Reformation or the French Revolution, nothing was left unaffected.

If the country as a whole witnessed great social change and upheaval, this crystallised in London. After the Great Fire of 1666, the city's geographical and social structure was transformed. The more affluent people saw an opportunity to start afresh so they migrated west and the poor that were left tended to migrate towards the east. As time moved on the population increased greatly, from 865,000 inhabitants in 1801 to 1.5 million by 1831. London became a city of contrasts.

1 Examine the ideas map below:

a Summarise each factor into one key point and add these to your own ideas map with the key question in the middle.

b Which of these factors do you think had the greatest impact on crime and policing in this period?

In the 1860s there were about 50,000 dress-makers and needlewomen employed in the West End of London. It was a seasonable trade and during which a twelve hour working day was common. Although some women and girls were employed on a permanent basis, most worked casually and their work had a very marked effect on their health… Their wages were rarely enough to live on… the majority were apt to drift into prostitution.

F. Sheppard, *London 1808–1870: The Infernal Wren*, 1971.

People

• the population of England increased from 10 million in 1750 to 42 million in 1900.

• London was the only great city in Britain in 1750 with a population of 675,000; this rose to over 3 million in 1900.

Economy

• income tax was first introduced during the 1790s to finance the expensive wars with France.

• when the Napoleonic Wars ended in 1815, taxation was given new impetus by the government and individuals like Sir Robert Peel to fund reforms.

Why did England change during the Industrial Revolution?

Government

• change had visited most corners of life in Britain and made the country into the most modern economy in the world. Governmental change did occur but it had to be fought for as you will find out later in the text.

• the French Revolution still echoed in the halls of Westminster so any sign of working class stirring kept MPs worried.

Rural to urban

• by 1750 most people lived in villages but by 1900 most of these lived in towns and cities.

• most towns in 1750 had become cities by 1900, e.g. Liverpool's population rose from 22,000 to 450,000; Manchester's from 18,000 to 376,000.

Social issues

• the influx of migrants from the countryside lead to overcrowding and poor living conditions.

• the gulf between rich and poor fuelled crime rates and fear of crime obsessed the rich. Newspapers – another new invention – spread sensational stories about highwaymen and murderers.

• unemployment peaked during the period, e.g. after the French wars when thousands of ex-soldiers came looking for work.

Wretched houses with broken windows patched with rags and paper, every room let out to a different family, and in many instances to two or even three – fruit and 'sweetstuff' manufacturers in the cellars, barbers and red-herring vendors in the front parlours, cobblers in the back; a bird-fancier in the first floor, three families in the second, starvation in the attics.

A description of St Giles Rookery by Charles Dickens in *Sketches by Boz*, 1839.

2 Read Source A and answer these questions:

What information does it give?

What guesses can I make? What can I infer?

What doesn't this source tell me?

What questions does it leave us with?

What else do I know to support my answer?

3 What can you find out from Source C about life in London in the 1800s?

4 Read Source D and compare it with Source B. Explain the image further using this new information.

Now, it's time to consider whether London in the 1800s really was an 'apocalypse of evil'.

5 Go through all of the sources and for each one answer the same questions that you asked about Source A above. Record your answers in a table.

1.14 Case study: Did the Fielding brothers win the 'War on Crime'?

LEARNING OBJECTIVES

In this lesson you will:
- learn about how the Fielding brothers started the first organised police force in Britain
- be able to demonstrate why law and order needed to improve.

What was law and order like before the Fielding brothers?

By the 1750s the population of London was about 650,000 and was increasing quickly. So was crime. Bringing an offender to justice during this time was generally done by the victims themselves and if they could not follow up an offence, the only alternative was to hire a thief-taker. This type of policing was open to abuse and the reputation of thief-takers was low mainly because of the infamous Jonathan Wild who from 1711 to 1725 had been the head of a criminal network in London whilst also holding office as the chief thief-catcher. The old Anglo-Saxon system of working as constable once a year still existed. Watchmen still operated but were regarded by most people as virtually useless at stopping crime, see Source A.

Evidently, policing was in need of reform. It was London that witnessed the major developments and proposals for police reform during the 18th century.

SOURCE A

The beats of many watchmen are so short that they take only five minutes to walk them; which, done twice in an hour, means that he is either fifty minutes in his box or, what is more frequent, they meet two or three times in conversation. Frequently they are employed in shutting up shops, or going on errands for the inhabitants or going into public houses with prostitutes. Also, from their practice of being fixed in a certain box for many years, there is no doubt some of them receive bribes from persons who commit robberies.

M. Wood, Lord Mayor of London.

The architects of these reforms were the brothers Henry and John Fielding.

Why did the Fielding brothers start a 'war on crime'?

The Fielding brothers took a much wider view of their mission to crack crime, unlike their forerunners. They believed that the rise in crime was only a symptom of a greater deep-rooted problem, a new society where self-interest and individualism were the most important things. They thought that prevention was as important as the cure of crime and that it could never be prevented unless an attempt was made to understand its causes.

ACTIVITY

1. You are a journalist for *The London Evening Post*, which has been informed that someone has started reforming the police in London. You have been assigned to do the first interview before any other newspaper. However, you can only ask five questions. Create a table with five headings: Who? What? When? Why? Where? Under each heading, write one question you would like to ask to find out about this new development in law and order.

Henry and John Fielding.

Fact file

Henry Fielding was a journalist and novelist who became London's magistrate at Bow Street in 1748 following De Veil who had originally created the office. Henry published his *Inquiry into the Causes of the Late Increase in Robbery* in 1751 in which he identified the main reasons for the increase as gambling and gin-drinking, because criminals needed to steal to fund their habits.

Sir John Fielding was appointed Henry's personal assistant in 1750. He eventually replaced his brother as Chief Magistrate of Bow Street in 1754. He had been blinded during a navy accident at the age of 19 and was sometimes known as 'The Blind Beak'. People at the time remarked on his hearing which was said to be so acute that he could recognise as many as 3000 criminals just by the sound of their voices.

How did John Fielding reform the police force?

Sir John Fielding believed that the 'war on crime' had to be fought where it was being committed.

He turned the Bow Street Office into a kind of police station with a group of trained and paid thief-takers. This new force would later be called the 'Bow Street Runners'. He also produced plans for a centralised police force in London with six separate police offices under the supervision of Bow Street, which would be used as a base for information-sharing. This was central to the war on crime.

Between 1772 and 1773, Fielding revealed his *General Preventative Plan*. The new plan built on his experiences in London and would make the Bow Street Office into a national crime information network. The plan received financial backing by the government to the sum of £400 per year. The information was collected, collated and circulated from Bow Street in a newspaper aptly named *The Hue & Cry*.

In 1775 Sir John Fielding came up with some new and more radical proposals.

- A system of paid professional police was needed.
- An increased number of petty constables was necessary.
- High constables living within 160 kilometres of London were to reside on the main road. These constables would also keep a sign outside announcing their position as police constables. If necessary, they would have to chase the offender and were given funds to pay for a horse.

Did the Fieldings pave the way for the modern-day police force?

This new plan received only lukewarm response from the government, not only because of the cumbersome work of reorganising city constables, but mainly because high constables were men of certain social standing and they would have been horrified at the prospect of having to chase a common criminal – that was the job of a thief-taker!

The actual word *police* was not to be found in English usage until 1714 and the idea of a paid professional police was alien to the political climate of the 1800s for many reasons:

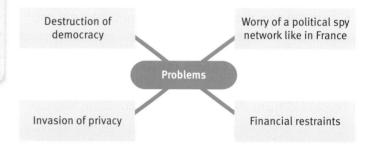

Destruction of democracy

Worry of a political spy network like in France

Problems

Invasion of privacy

Financial restraints

ACTIVITY

2 Using your five questions table as well as other research, complete a fishbone diagram like the one below.
   - Each light blue box is a reason or factor.
   - Each line serves as a key point for that reason or factor.
   - Together they answer the question.
   - You can add as many extra lines as you need.
   - When you have completed your research, compare your findings with a partner and add any additional details to your fishbone diagram.

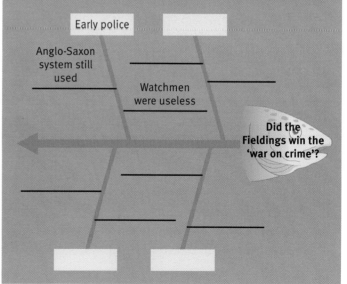

Early police

Anglo-Saxon system still used

Watchmen were useless

Did the Fieldings win the 'war on crime'?

1.15 What part did Robert Peel play in the establishment of a police force in Britain?

The Government takes control of law enforcement

The period from the end of the Napoleonic Wars to the 1840s witnessed unprecedented economic, political and social unrest, which terrified the landed ruling classes who saw subversion and revolution in every corner. The debate for combating crime and protest took a new turn.

When Sir Robert Peel was appointed Home Secretary in 1822 he was well aware of strong feelings against the creation of a new police force. He also knew that the existing system of policing was failing and that the general public had lost faith in it, particularly after events such as the Peterloo Massacre seen in Source A.

SOURCE A

Engraving of the events in Manchester: yeomanry are ordered to clear a crowd gathered to hear speeches supporting parliamentary reform. Eleven people die, about 400 are injured (1819).

Fear of revolution

Landowners, the vast majority of which were MPs, were deeply concerned that the wind of the French Revolution would spread to Britain. The protests of the early 1800s suggested that this was possible.

What factors led to the need for a police force?

Taxation

Income tax had first been introduced as a temporary tax in 1799 to pay for the Napoleonic Wars. This tax was re-introduced in 1842 by Peel himself. Local authorities were also allowed to raise taxes.

The army

The army was still used to establish order in most areas. This had already proven disastrous:
- Gordon Riots – soldiers opened fire and killed 100s of people
- Peterloo Massacre – cavalry used sabres to cut through protestors.

Inefficient system

Constables and watchmen could not handle the crime increase which had resulted from the Industrial Revolution. The Bloody Code (see Chapter 3) or the Penal code was unproductive and did not deter people from committing offences.

1 Examine Source A. What impression do you get about the public's attitude towards policing almost 40 years after the Fielding brothers' reforms?

2 What do you think Peel needs to do to change the public's attitude? In pairs, write down nine things you feel the police should do.

3 Examine Source C. Why do you think the police had such a uniform? What was the thought behind it?

4 As you read through the rest of this lesson, think about this: many of the Fielding brothers' proposals were not accepted. Why did Peel manage to succeed where the Fieldings did not?

London's done – what next?

1835: *The Municipal Corporation Act* gave boroughs the authority to establish police forces paid from their rates.

1839: Bow Street Runners were abolished and the MPF took over their duties.

1842: Detective branch was set up whose task was to detect crime.

1856: *The County Rural Police Act* made it compulsory for all towns and counties to have a police force.

1878: Criminal Investigation Department (CID) was set up to investigate crimes of a more serious nature.

Fact file

The duties of Peel's new Metropolitan Police Force (MPF), 'Bobbies' or 'Peelers' as they were sometimes called, were restricted to London at first. The very high turnover during the first few years was suggestive of the stress involved in creating this new police.

How effective were the Peelers?

Although there is no real way of measuring the success of the police there are a few pointers that suggest that they were successful. The presence of Peelers on the streets of London seemed to deter criminals and crime rates decreased sharply between 1829 and 1835. However, this did not mean that offenders disappeared as many criminals moved their activities to nearby towns. The responsibility of bringing prosecutions to court became that of the police and coupled with the decrease in crime led to general public acceptance of the new force. Public attitude did however change gradually as you will find out in the next lesson.

SOURCE B

Police... should maintain a relationship with the public that gives reality to the historic tradition that the police are the public and the public are the police; the police being only members of the public who are paid to give full-time attention to duties which are... in the interests of community...

Peelian Principles, Principle no. 7.

SOURCE C

In those days... they [wore] swallow-tail blue coats, with bright metal buttons, and in summer, white duck trousers and white Berlin gloves. In lieu of a helmet they had an ordinary chimney-pot hat, only of extra strength and stiffness, and with a glazed oilskin hat...

Edmund Yates, *His Recollections and Experiences*, 1885.

Fact file

Sir Robert Peel (1788–1850) was Conservative Prime Minister from 1834 to 1835, and again from 1841 to 1846. His government passed a number of social reforms including the Factory Act of 1844, which limited working hours for children and women in factories, and the Gaols Act (1823), which built on earlier reforms.

Initially Peel focused his attention on reforming the criminal law which few people were concerned about, and carefully used this issue to develop his credibility and his allies. When he finally revealed that although the population had only increased by $15\frac{1}{2}$ per cent between 1822 and 1828 but that crime had increased by 40 per cent, few could dispute that action was necessary. The Metropolitan Police Bill met hardly any opposition and became law in 1829.

Sir Robert Peel set out his *Peelian Principles* (or *Peel's Nine Principles*), which defined the ethical requirements police officers must follow in order to be effective (see Source B).

VOICE YOUR OPINION!

The story of law and order in Britain has been one of gradual change. The Bow Street Runners and the Metropolitan Police were needed because of certain factors. What factors do you think our police force has been affected by?

1.16 Why did some people fear Peel's new police force?

LEARNING OBJECTIVES

In this lesson, you will:
- recall key facts about why the police faced such opposition
- categorise key factors and explain their importance.

The public's attitude towards the newly formed police force ranged from fear and bitterness to violent anger. This only changed when it was evident that the police had made a significant contribution to the decrease in crime. Meanwhile, several attempts were made to win over the public. The police uniform of top hats and blue swallow tailed suits, tried to make them look more like civilians and less like the traditional army. Much time was also spent cleansing the force of poor quality officers, which meant, for example, sacking those who drank or took bribes.

Fact file

Approximately 50 per cent of the constables in the new-found force were sacked for drunkenness and disorderly behaviour.

A cruel satire aimed at the Commissioners of Police features a skeleton in a policeman's uniform moving on a starving, homeless woman and her baby. *The Tomahawk* magazine, 1867.

SOURCE B

WHERE CAN THE POLICE BE?

Where can the police be? G. Cruikshank in *Comic Almanack*, 1847.

SOURCE C

Many people feared that 'Peel's Bloody Gang' would become a private army of the government.

D. Brandon, *Stand and Deliver*, 2004.

For radicals, the police was neither 'of the people' or 'for the people' but a third political force (after the government and the judiciary) working on behalf of the land-owning classes.

C. Emsley, *Crime and Society in England*, 2004.

SOURCE

According to PC Henry Wood, in his written report dated 29th April 1834, he joined the force on 25th March that year. He was issued with his uniform at Scotland Yard and then walked to Poplar police station to which he was posted. He was there instructed of his duties and the next night found him walking his beat… as a fully-fledged constable.

C. Bloom, *Violent London*, 2004.

SOURCE

The New Police

PARISHIONERS, ~ ask yourselves the following Questions:
Why is an Englishman, if he complains of an outrage or an insult, referred for redress to a Commissioner of Police?
Why is a Commissioner of Police delegated to administer Justice?
Why are the proceedings of this new POLICE COURT unpublished and unknown? and by what Law of the Land is it recognized?
Why is the British Magistrate stripped of his power? and why is Justice transferred from the Justice Bench?
Why is the Sword of Justice placed in the hands of a MILITARY Man?

Consider these constitutional questions : consider the additional burthen saddled on you ~ consider all these points, then UNITE in removing such a powerful force from the hands of Government, and let us institute a Police System in the hands of the PEOPLE under parochial appointments ~

UNITY IS STRENGTH ; THEREFORE,

I.~Let each Parish convene a Meeting.
II.~Let a Committee be chosen, instructed to communicate with other Parishes.
III.~Let Delegates be elected from each Committee to form a CENTRAL COMMITTEE.

To join your Brother Londoners in one heart, one hand for the Abolition of the New Police!

ELLIOT, Printer, 14, Holywell Street, Strand.

This poster, from 1830, raises various objections and calls for public meetings to 'Abolish the New Police!'. National Archives: HO 61/2.

SOURCE

One of the duties of the police was to protect property, that is, land and estates.

C. Emsley, *Crime and Society in England*, 2004.

SOURCE

Satire remarking on the incompetence of the police with reference to the Jack the Ripper murder enquiry. Blind man's buff. *Punch*, 22 September 1888.

ACTIVITY

1   The aim of this activity is to investigate key factors (reasons) why some people disliked or perhaps even feared Sir Robert Peel's new police force. Some of these key factors could for example be the *government* or the *belief that the new recruits were incompetent*.

Examine Sources A–H and work out which key factors would be useful in answering the question: **Why did some people fear Peel's new police force?** Then create a Venn diagram using the key factors as headings. Put evidence from Sources A–H into your Venn diagram and make a separate list of any evidence that does not match one of your headings. Do these provide any more factors you could add?

1.17 How has policing developed since the 19th century?

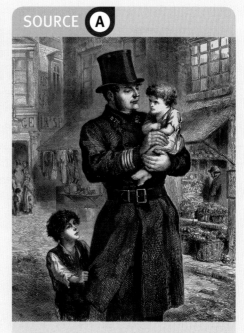

SOURCE A

A late 19th-century depiction of a policeman.

What were the key turning points in the history of policing in Britain?

You have studied the development of law and the origins of law and order and will have noticed that the development was one of gradual change. What started as a community-based system with the Fielding brothers gradually changed until it became the centrally controlled Metropolitan Police Force in 1829. The nationally organised professional force of the 19th century continued to progress at a steady pace and faced many challenges along the way.

The organisation and methods of crime fighting in the 19th century varied from force to force and there was little contact or cooperation between them. There was also no centralised system for criminal record-keeping which made it more challenging to coordinate action against criminals who could move virtually unnoticed from town to town.

Police duties during this time ranged from inspecting registered lodging-houses, extinguishing fires, to patrolling 12 hours a day, covering an area of almost 20 miles. Apart from taking statements from people or requesting a **post-mortem**, after murders for example, there was very little the police could do to catch criminals unless they were caught red-handed.

You might have noticed how some improvements came about as a consequence of changes in society and that some did not work as well as others. You have also had the opportunity to investigate changes and continuities in law and order across time as well as explore the reasons why Sir Robert Peel managed to succeed in developing the first national police force in Britain. You will now examine the key turning points in the history of crime prevention in Britain and make a judgement about each one.

SOURCE B

Metropolitan Police recruitment poster for more police around 1930s.

KEY WORDS

Post-mortem – *from the Latin meaning 'after death'; medical examination of a corpse.*

VOICE YOUR OPINION!

Police nowadays have negative nicknames like 'Fuzz' or 'Pigs', but these tend to be used by younger generations. In the 1820s both adults and children used derogative terms such as 'Blue Devils' and 'Peel's Bloody Gang' to describe the first police.

1 Why do you think the police force became more acceptable to people later in the 19th century?

2 Why do some people today regard the police in a negative way?

SOURCE **C**

Metropolitan Police at the end of the 1990s.

ACTIVITY

2 Using the ideas map below, create a table similar to this one and examine how some aspects of police work, for example communication or transport, changed between 1850 and the 20th century.

Aspects of police work	Evidence of change	What impact did this have on policing?

1850		20th Century
The Metropolitan Police appointed a small group of full-time detectives in the 1840s. People believed these officers were more corruptible than ordinary policemen so this body was increased only slowly.	**Specialisation**	The police have set up a number of specialist forces to handle particular issues, e.g. the Criminal Investigation Department (1877); Fingerprints Branch (1901); 1920 women were appointed; or the Anti-Terrorist (or Bomb) Squad (1971).
Communication was an issue. 'Conference points' were arranged for officers patrolling neighbouring beats so they could meet up and exchange information. In towns, officers carried whistles and were ordered to remain within whistle call of each other.	**Communication**	Dr Crippen was the first criminal to be caught using radio communication, namely the telegraph (1910). Other inventions that helped shape the way the police operates have been: telephones (1901), police phone boxes (1920s), 999 call in 1937.
The police were unarmed and travelled on foot apart from the Thames River Police.	**Transport and weapons**	The police remain unarmed unless they have been equipped with firearms at airports or belong to specialist units. Most officers now carry extendable batons and CS or PAVA spray. Bicycles were first used in 1909, radios in 1910, cars in 1919 (but only used widely from the 1930s).
In 1900 there were 60,000 police officers in approx. 190 forces with their own rules, wages and conditions.	**Power and organisation**	In 2000, there were 41 forces in Britain and over 125,000 police officers.
In 1900 recruits learnt on the job and pay was poor, for example, in Staffordshire police constables were paid seventeen shillings a week (the equivalent of 70 pence).	**Training and duties**	A National Police College was set up in 1947 to provide further training. Today, each police officer has 14 weeks training and the pay is good.

GradeStudio

Putting it all together

You have now completed this unit, which has focused on the development of law enforcement from Roman times to today. You have also had practice in answering questions designed to prepare you for your exam. Below is an example of one type of exam question, with some hints to help you write a top-scoring answer.

a Explain why Sir Robert Peel was able to set up a police force in the late 1820s. **[7 marks]**

Examiner's tip

Explanation questions often begin with a simple 'why' or 'explain why', and then add a situation. This question is actually asking you to explain the factors behind the situation, i.e. the reasons why the change or event took place.

Before you answer the question, look carefully at some of the issues that could be worth thinking about in the chart below. Then read the candidate's answer. Using the chart and the simplified mark scheme, can you spot why the candidate moved up the levels?

What should I write about?	Exemplar answer	Structure and tips
Introduction Law and order before Robert Peel began his work Explanation of why change was needed	For example, '*Robert Peel managed to set up the Metropolitan Police Force in 1829 as he managed to improve earlier systems of policing and received financial as well as political backing from the government.*'	Make your argument clear right from the start. It makes your writing more organised and the examiner will know the direction of your writing.
PARAGRAPH 1 Problems with old system Work of the Fieldings	For example, '*The old system of law and order was breaking down. Constables were corrupt and a police force was needed because nobody was catching the criminals. Peel managed to build on earlier systems of crime prevention…*'	Write about each of the points and explain why law and order were not working. At the end of your paragraph, create a mini-conclusion by referring back to the question and say why Peel was able to set up the police.
PARAGRAPH 2 Other reasons Other factors that led to the setting up of a police force, like taxation and Peel's ability The importance of these factors	For example, '*Peel's influence as Home Secretary and financial backing were also crucial for setting up the Police. Peel made sure that…*'	Write about each of the points and explain what other factors help to explain why Peel managed to set up the new police force. At the end of your paragraph, create a mini-conclusion by referring back to the question.
CONCLUSION Your opinion on the factors and which are most important What evidence you have to back up the conclusion you reach	For example, '*The Fieldings were important in showing that a police force was needed. This inspired Peel to set up the Metropolitan Police in 1829. However, there were other factors, like taxation and Peel's own ability. These added…*'	Try to make a judgement: what other attempts had been made prior to Robert Peel? Why did Peel succeed where others did not?

Level 1:
General comment without specific contextual knowledge

Level 2:
Identifies specific reasons but does not explain

Level 3:
Explains one specific reason

Level 4:
Explains more than one specific reason

... *Peel set up the first widespread police force because he felt Britain needed to deal with crime.* Peel believed that previous systems, e.g. the Bow Street Runners or watchmen, no longer worked and crime had increased quickly because of the Industrial Revolution. Also, he was able to set up the police force as he had the **backing of the government as income tax had been introduced in 1799 to finance the Napoleonic Wars**, unlike the Fielding brothers for example who used private finances to pay for the Bow Street Runners. Also, the government and the landowners were **terrified that a revolution similar to the one in France** would happen in Britain so they agreed that something had to be done ...

Swap answers with a partner. Using the mark scheme, see if you can spot when they move into Levels 3–4.

Simplified mark scheme

Level 1   Makes general assertions OR describes Peel's police force.   **[1 mark]**
          Valid but general answers. No specific contextual knowledge.
          For example, '*He thought a police force was needed because nobody was catching the criminals. They were getting away with it and so something had to be done.*'

Level 2   Identifies specific reasons.   **[2–3 marks]**
          Specific contextual knowledge demonstrated but no explanation.
          For example, '*inefficiency of present systems like the watchmen and constables, industrialisation/rapid growth of towns, rise in crime, fear of riots/protest, greater involvement of government in everyday life, people getting used to paying taxes for things like this*'.

Level 3   Explains one specific reason.   **[4–6 marks]**
          For example, *Peel was able to set up a police force because many people were afraid of popular protests and even revolution. This was just after the French Revolution and they were afraid the same thing would happen here especially after riots like the Luddites and Peterloo. Rich people thought that a police force would protect their property and wealth and keep law and order.*

Level 4   Explains more than one specific reason.   **[7 marks]**
          Give six marks for one reason explained and another identified.
          Give top marks for two reasons explained.

Now plan and write your own answer. Refer to the chart and the simplified mark scheme to help you achieve the full seven marks available for this question.

2.1 Crime: Four eras of 'violent Britain'?

On 13 March 1964 Kitty Genovese was stabbed to death near her home without any interruptions in a busy residential area. It was estimated that at least 38 people witnessed her murder taking place in one way or another but did nothing to prevent it happening. None of these witnesses were ever taken to court for not stopping this crime being committed. On 17 April 2009 a court in Sweden jailed four men behind The Pirate Bay, the world's most high-profile file-sharing website, in a landmark case. They were fined £3.5 million and sentenced to one year in prison. These are both examples of crimes yet we perceive them differently. The murder is easy to deal with for all of us, but is the case of the witnesses straightforward? What about the file-sharing of music, videos and other digital media, is that ok? Would the British government agree or disagree, and why is that?

You will become familiar with a range of different types of crimes in this section and why some of these disappear whilst others continue and even develop into newer versions of an older crime. When you study this next theme, consider the different types of crime:

- Crimes against the person: murder, armed robbery, violent crime and sexual crimes like rape.
- Crimes against property: poaching, smuggling, piracy, theft, burglary and theft of horses and sheep.
- Crimes against authority: conspiracy, heresy, treason and witchcraft.

SOURCE A

Teenagers are downing alcohol as if it is fizzy pop as incidents of drink-fuelled violence and rape soar, a chief constable told MPs yesterday... he warned that the number of rapes related to alcohol is on the rise, and alcohol was a factor in nearly half of violent crime last year. This compares to only a third of violent attacks in 2004–5, the year before Labour allowed pubs and clubs to open 24 hours.

Daily Mail, 4 June 2008.

SOURCE B

NOTWITHSTANDING THE INSINUATIONS OF A CERTAIN STIPENDIARY—JONES IS *NOT* AFRAID OF HIS SHADOW.

" *Now, then, you Scoundrel—I know what you're at—and if you're not off, I'll Shoot you!* "

A newspaper cartoon from 1862 commenting on the garrotting panic.

Nineteenth-century killers: Media-generated panic or reality?

Gangs of youngsters control the streets!

10,000 knife-crimes per year!

Mary Ann Cotton: child killer

Read the headlines carefully. They have been taken from actual crimes committed either during the 1800s or in 2008.

- Can you spot which ones belong in 1800 and 2008 respectively?
- How far do you think the media is the cause of some public panics?
- What crimes are 'popular' to write about? Can you identify what factors are linked to these particular crimes? For example: Murder – personal safety.

Was crime on the increase in the late 1800s?

On the morning of Tuesday, 15 November 1892 Dr Thomas Neill Cream was executed in London's Newgate Prison. Dr Cream was the sort of criminal who makes headlines and sells newspapers. He was a serial killer who had murdered seven women in Britain and the United States. He was the sort of criminal who, by his crimes, seemed both mad and evil. Dr Cream was the kind of criminal that the public wanted criminals to be. Outside the prison crowds waited in the rain to spot the black flag winched up which was the signal that the Doctor had been executed. They cheered when it was raised: 'Now "ee's a-hangin"' was apparently shouted out. How typical was Dr Cream of Victorian criminals?

The industrial period witnessed a major shift in attitudes towards the poor, particularly during the Napoleonic Wars and immediately after. Most importantly, in the aftermath of the Gordon Riots and the French Revolution, there was a sense of fear amongst the landed ruling classes that the 'criminal classes' and working classes were organising themselves in the towns. For evidence of this, they needed only to look, for example, to the Chartists (1838–48) or the Tolpuddle Martyrs of 1834 (see pages 118–119). Many people in the property-owning classes, some of whom were politicians, believed that the poor were poor because of their immorality and lack of self control. At the end of the wars in 1815, men of property cheered at the abolition of income tax, but the increase in local poor rates showed no signs of declining.

The garroting panic

'Garotting' was the popular term for street robbery or what we nowadays call 'mugging'. Garotting, by definition, refers to the method of killing by strangulation or breaking the neck of a victim and was known to be used from the 1st century BC in Rome. The 1862 panic began when an MP was robbed on his way home from a late sitting of the House of Commons. The press began to see garrotters everywhere, and entrepreneurs with an eye for the main chance began marketing 'anti-garotte collars' and fierce, lead-weighted 'life-preservers' for gentlemen out after dark. Nevertheless the number of garottings during the main panic seems to have been rather small:

- 2 in September
- 12 in October
- 32 in November
- 14 in December

These figures tell us more about the pattern of the panic than any reality in the incidence of the crime. In fact, much of the panic appears to have been generated and maintained by the press, notably the influential *Times*, which was seeking tougher punishment for offenders. Yet the vast majority of the people who appeared before the courts of Victorian England had committed neither murder nor robbery with violence. Most offenders were young men charged with petty theft, who did not have detailed plans of theft, but stole when the occasion presented itself.

As you work through this chapter, keep in mind the big question:

Has violent crime in Britain become worse over the centuries?

When you reach the end of the chapter, note down your thoughts about the big question. Try to make a judgement, giving your reasons.

SOURCE C

A 19th-century cartoon highlighting the fear felt by the middle classes at the reported rise in muggings or 'garottings'.

2.2 How accurate were Juvenal's comments about crime in Rome?

LEARNING OBJECTIVES

In this lesson you will:
- begin to understand how interpretations are constructed
- draw information together to create a conclusion.

There are no records or statistics that tell us about crime in Ancient Rome. However, the laws created in the Twelve Tables and by Emperors like Justinian (see page 5) must have reflected the crimes that were being committed. Rome had to deal with a whole range of crimes from people who were both rich and poor; crimes could be as serious as rebellion or as common as petty theft.

In Source C the Roman satirist Juvenal comments on crime in Ancient Rome. Satirists like to poke fun at real-life subjects by exaggerating them in order to make people laugh. However, the humour only works if you can see that it is based on actual events and problems. This leaves historians with an important question: how much is based on facts and observation and how much is exaggeration to make people laugh?

SOURCE B

The petty thieves support Vatia for the election.

A copper pot is missing from this shop. 65 sesterces reward if anybody brings it back, 20 sesterces if he reveals the thief so we can get our property back.

Take your lewd looks and flirting eyes off another man's wife, and show some decency on your face!

I am yours for 2 asses cash.

Translations of graffiti found on walls in Pompeii. *Asses* and *sesterces* were types of Roman coins.

GETTING STARTED

Look at Source A.

What is the message behind this graffiti?

Is it possible to be funny and serious at the same time?

Is all graffiti like this? Why?

SOURCE A

'Stop and Search' a piece of artwork by the artist Banksy.

ACTIVITIES

1 Source B includes several examples of messages found on the city walls of Pompeii. What do they reveal about crime in the Roman Empire?

2 What crimes and problems did Rome have? Are they similar to those faced by cities today?

3 Your task is to decide whether Juvenal's opinions are accurate. Read Source C carefully, compare it to the other sources and then draw some conclusions about the accuracy of the account.

For what can you do, when he that gives the command is mad with drink, and at the same time stronger than you! 'Where do you come from?' he thunders out: 'With whose vinegar and beans are you blown out? What cobbler has been feasting on chopped leek or boiled sheep's head with you? Don't you answer? Speak, or be kicked! Say where do you hang out? In what Jew's begging-stand shall I look for you?' Whether you attempt to say a word or retire in silence, is all one; they beat you just the same, and then, in a passion, force you to give bail to answer for the assault. This is a poor man's liberty! When thrashed he humbly begs, and pummelled with fisticuffs supplicates to be allowed to quit the spot with a few teeth left in his head.

Nor is this yet all that you have to fear, for there will not be wanting one to rob you, when all the houses are shut up, and all the fastenings of the shops chained, are fixed and silent. Sometimes too a footpad does your business with his knife...

Extract from Juvenal's *Satire III*, about 100 CE.

Those who commit capital crimes are, if from the upper classes, decapitated or exiled; those from the lower orders are crucified, burnt alive or thrown to the beasts.

Extract from a legal manual c.300 BCE.

While praetor, he openly took bribes offered to influence his verdict when presiding over murder trials – so openly that the following year it was decided to launch an inquiry. Tubulus, however, fled the country forthwith, without daring to defend himself – it was an open and shut case.

Extract from *On Moral Ends* by Cicero regarding the case of Lucius Hostilius Tubulus in 141 BCE. Tubulus was brought back to Rome to face charges and imprisoned, but took poison before he could be tried.

Roman ruin: Why people committed crime

1. *Hunger*
Crops frequently failed and bad harvests led to thousands of people having no food and no money to buy it.

2. *Alcohol*
Drinking was popular and frequent. Fights and sexual assaults regularly occurred after people had been drinking.

3. *Sport*
The Roman historian Tacitus tells how sports fans clashed in Pompeii in 59 CE. Sporting rivalry caused fights.

4. *Big cities*
The development of big cities led to crowded streets and the dark alleyways that gave opportunity for criminals to work and hide.

5. *Conquest*
The Roman Empire conquered many lands and took many slaves. This led local people to rebel against their rule.

ACTIVITIES

The five factors opposite are those that historians believe caused crime in Ancient Rome.

4 Rank order the causes – number 1 should be the factor that you think would have caused the most crime and 5 the least. Explain your order by writing a sentence about why you have placed the causes in those positions.

5 Decide which of the five causes have some link to the account of crime given by Juvenal (Source C). Read carefully and think about the type of people committing crime.

6 In this lesson, you have looked at the account of crime in Rome by Juvenal. Make a list of the five key points he makes about crime. Now, compare this list to the graffiti of Pompeii, the other sources and the causes of crime historians have suggested. How many of Juvenal's claims are backed up by the other evidence? Can you say why this might be?

2.3 Case study: Murder in Rome

In this lesson you will:

- learn about serious crime in the Roman Empire
- practise writing answers to interpretation questions.

KEY WORDS

Senate – *political institution.*
Tribune – *political leader.*

Several accounts of murders in Ancient Rome have survived to this day. Here is a selection of some of them.

ACTIVITY

1 Read the accounts carefully and then create an ideas map using words and images to show the reasons why these murders were committed.

Story 1: The legend of Horatius

Horatius fought alongside his two brothers in the Roman Army and helped to defeat the Etruscan forces. When he returned home, he saw his sister sobbing because the Etruscan she had loved was killed in the fighting. Horatius was so angry with her that he drew his sword and stabbed her. He then said, 'So perish any Roman woman who mourns for an enemy.' Horatius was put on trial and condemned to death. His father appealed for him and he was later pardoned.

Story 2: Killing tribunes

In 133 BCE a **tribune** called Tiberius Gracchus, who was trying to reform Rome, was clubbed to death by his opponents in the **Senate**. Nine years later his brother suffered the same fate for the same reason. In 100 BCE another tribune, Lucius Saturninus, was assassinated after the Senate passed an emergency decree against him.

Story 3: Sextus Roscius and the mystery gang

In 80 BCE Sextus Roscius was returning home after a dinner party when he was attacked by a group of men. The main suspect appeared to be the man's son, also called Sextus Roscius. In court he was defended by a brilliant lawyer called Cicero.

He managed to convince the court that the killer was a freed slave who used to work for Sulla – a rival of the family. Roscius was acquitted; this was a lucky escape because the punishment for killing your father was to be sewn into a large sack with a snake, a cockerel, a dog and a monkey before being tossed into the nearest river.

Story 4: Massacre in Spain

In 150 BCE the governor of Spain, Servius Sulpicius Galba, found his army in a conflict against the Lusitanians. Faking friendship he asked them to abandon their weapons and join him for talks. No sooner had they thrown their weapons in a ditch, he ordered a group of legionnaires to attack and kill them all. This event caused outrage in Rome.

Story 5: Something sounds fishy!

Publius Vedius Pollio discovered that a slave had accidentally broken a valuable goblet in his house. He ordered that he be thrown into a pond of man-eating lampreys.

ACTIVITIES

2 Why do you think that it is these stories that writers of the day decided to tell people about?

3 Why do we have few accounts of murder as the result of robbery, or of ordinary people committing crimes of passion?

4 Do the stories reveal more about Ancient Rome, or the kind of events people liked to read about?

5 Can you see something similar happening in the news today? What types of murder do we hear about? What impression of society does that give?

By now, you should have a good understanding of crime in Ancient Rome. You have also been practising a key skill needed to achieve at GCSE: interpretation. This exercise will help you to plan out and write a top-level answer for the following exam question:

'Crime was commonplace… the city [of Rome] was plagued with housebreakers, pickpockets, petty thieves and muggers.' How far does this source and evidence above support this impression? Explain your answer using the sources and your own knowledge. **[5 marks]**

Examiner's tip

Source questions usually begin with: 'How far… ?' For this type of question, there are two main aspects to think about.
- Always have some statements that support and some that contradict the opinion given in the question.
- The words 'How far… ' are prompting you to make a judgement about the amount of accuracy. Your conclusion is important.

This table is to help you structure your first source question. Use the guidance in all three columns to help you to build your answer. Once you have looked carefully at the question and the table, try to write an answer of your own.

What should I write about?	My answer	Structure and tips
PARAGRAPH 1 Juvenal creates an accurate impression of Rome Many violent crimes Problems of big cities. Alcohol problems	For example, '*This source does give an accurate impression of crime.* *At the time Juvenal was writing, 100 CE, the Roman Empire had grown and it had many large cities. City life had benefits, but there was also a high level of crime. For example, groups of young men caused trouble in the streets after they had been drinking. Also…*'	Write about each point in detail – this moves you into higher marks. At the end of your paragraph, create a mini-conclusion by referring back to the question.
PARAGRAPH 2 Juvenal's account was not accurate Was many murders Writers concentrate on high profile crimes Juvenal is satirist, his job is to exaggerate	For example, '*This source does not give an accurate impression of crime.* *Not all Romans were murderers like this, they were just ordinary people who did not have much money, but led honest lives. These people do not have their stories told because working in a fish market or mending shoes is not as exciting to write about as murders and drunken brawls. Cicero was happy to talk about his cases when they involved violent acts, because this attracted the readers.*'	If you can use your contextual knowledge (knowledge of the time the source was written) to support and criticise your statement you will reach the highest level. At the end of your paragraph, create a mini-conclusion by referring back to the question.
Conclusion Judgement Supporting evidence Key point	For example, '*Juvenal's account shows that Rome had problems and the evidence suggests that he is right. In any big city there will be crime, simply because there are lots of people, busy streets and more opportunities to commit crimes. Other writers support his view with tales of gang killings, armed robbery and assassinations, for example the murder in 80 CE of Sextus Roscius. However, as a satirist, Juvenal would need to make an extreme point of view to grab the attention of his audience. He therefore…*'	Try to make a judgement: how accurate is the source? Was it more accurate than not, or are the flaws too serious? Can you explain your position on the source? Are there one or two factors for this that are more important than the others? Why?

2.4 Was Anglo-Saxon society riddled with crime?

LEARNING OBJECTIVES

In this lesson you will:
- explain change and continuity over time
- analyse a variety of problems faced by Anglo-Saxon kings.

Anglo-Saxon kingdoms and the people in charge were not so different from our own: if we want to find out the issues that troubled people then we can look at the laws that they were making. Rulers will make laws that reflect the major concerns in society, just like the British government in response to the London terrorist attacks.

Anglo-Saxon laws reveal that kings were most worried about theft, but were also concerned with **treason** and violence against citizens. Treason is a problem just for rulers, but the other two could affect anyone in society. In early Saxon times, kings tended to leave alone issues that did not directly affect them. Therefore, crime tended to be settled by **bleudfeud**. Kings only looked at unusual cases, like when a man without relatives was killed, where there was no one to pursue the criminal for compensation.

However, several factors helped to change the mind of kings and make them become more involved in dealing with crime. One important factor was religion. In around 690 the King of Wessex, Ine, introduced three new crimes: not being baptised, not going to church on Sunday and not paying church taxes. Ordinary people could be fined if they committed any of these crimes. Once the Saxon leaders converted to Christianity they wanted their people to do the same.

King Alfred (871–99 CE) had many crimes to deal with. Read the information in the boxes to see just some of his major concerns.

GETTING STARTED

The most significant laws to be made in 2006 were those regarding terrorism. The government entered into a long battle with other political parties and the House of Lords to increase the amount of time that terror suspects could be held without charge to 48 days. The government said that terrorism was the most important issue of the time and that steps had to be taken to help the police stop it.

Terrorism is not a new phenomenon, so why was the government anxious to change the law towards it?

Story 1

Kings committing crimes against kings

Alfred's older brother, Aethelred, had been King of Wessex before him (866–71). According to the family will, Aethelred's son was passed over for the throne and Alfred became king in 871. The son, Aethelwold, seems to have accepted this situation. However, Aethelwold must have had some supporters, because Alfred mentions him and his supporters, linking them to treason. When Alfred died in 899 he was succeeded by his son Edward. Aethelwold was furious and staged a revolt against the new king. He went to the Vikings in Northumbria for support and they made him their king. Next he raised a Viking army in East Anglia and led them against his cousin, Edward. Aethelwold was killed in the Battle of the Holme in 903 and the revolt was ended.

Story 2

Lords committing crimes against kings

In a charter of 901 is the story of Ealdorman Wulfhere. He lost his lands in Wiltshire 'when he deserted both his lord King Alfred and his country, in spite of the oath which he had sworn to the King.' It is known that Wulfhere was a supporter of Aethelwold's father and it is quite likely that he was involved in Aethelwold's revolt in 899.

After Alfred's time new laws reveal a growing number of crimes and although treason is mentioned, other crimes seem to have a higher priority.

Aethelstan and theft

After crushing Aethelwold's revolt, Edward's reign was secure. He turned his attention to other matters. The most important seems to have been theft of important goods. Edward ordered that all buying and selling of goods should be done in a port, where the process could be checked by a **reeve**. This was done to reduce theft, particularly of cattle.

As trade grew, so did confidence in the system and by the reign of Aethelstan (924–39) the law was relaxed and only the sale of goods valued at over 20 pence needed to be seen by a reeve. In addition, the king made sure that tithings understood that it was their duty to form a posse if there were cattle rustlers in the area. Families were also ordered to hand over thieves.

Edmund and runaway slaves

Edmund (939–59) issued a law that stated tithings had to round up **thralls** who had run away and become bandits. Many bandits existed and some slaves ran to the Vikings. If they were caught, few were killed; it was important that lords were able to keep them for working.

ACTIVITIES

1 What do stories 1 and 2 reveal about crime in Alfred's England?

2 Imagine that you were a monk at the time and needed to write a quick summary of crime around 890–905. Write a paragraph of no more than 40 words that answers the five Ws:

- WHO was committing crime?
- WHAT were they doing?
- WHEN?
- WHERE?
- WHY?

3 Now try to answer the question asked at the beginning of this lesson: Was Anglo-Saxon society riddled with crime?

To help you, look at all the social groups and use the evidence in this lesson to see if they committed crimes. Also, think about why these particular actions were made a crime by the rulers of the day – what are they trying to stop or control?

Complete a table like the one below to help gather your thoughts. An example has been done to help you.

Social group	Possible crimes committed	Why this action was made a crime
Kings		
Lords		
Merchants		
Peasants	Not being baptised Not attending church Not paying church taxes	The rulers were Christian and wanted their subjects to be as well.
Slaves		

2.5 Does the legend of Robin Hood reflect the reality of medieval outlaws?

LEARNING OBJECTIVES

In this lesson you will:

- learn about the legend of Robin Hood and medieval crime
- begin to explore how historians can use interpretations.

GETTING STARTED

Working with a partner, take it in turns to list things that you associate with the legend of Robin Hood. How many different things did you list?

Robin Hood and his Merry Men were outlaws and robbers who stole from the rich and gave to the poor while living in hiding in Sherwood Forest. That is the tradition that has been passed down and survives to this day. The legend is still being told and retold (see Source A).

The details of the stories themselves have changed over the years, but the same basic ideas still persist. The stories often revolve around the punishing of wrongdoers and those who are greedy, who often hold positions of authority; and the assisting of people in need, often peasants and women.

A good outlaw?

However, the legends detail many crimes that Robin and his men were said to have committed. Alongside robbery and poaching, Robin and his men murder and behead Guy of Gisbourne, who has come to arrest Robin; and in another story, Little John and Much murder a monk who has informed on Robin Hood, and the monk's servant to prevent him identifying the outlaws.

The first recorded mention of Robin Hood appears to be in 1262, when an outlawed man in Berkshire was given the nickname 'Robehod'. He is referred to again in the great 14th-century poem, *Piers Plowman*. Even as late as 1605, the Gunpowder plotters were referred to as 'Robin Hoods' due to their illegal activities. Robin Hood is now traditionally placed as living in the late 12th century during the absence of Richard I, who was taking part in the crusades.

SOURCE A

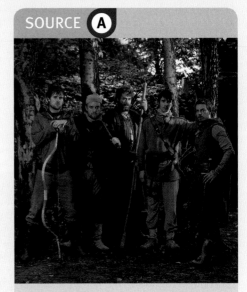

Robin Hood from the 2006 BBC drama series.

SOURCE B

'Therof no force,' than sayde Robyn;	*'Thereof no force,' then said Robin*
'We shall do well inowe;	*'We shall do well enough;*
But loke ye do no husbonde harme,	*But look you do no husband harm*
That tilleth with his ploughe.	*That tills with his plough.*
Cryst haue mercy on his soule,	*Christ have mercy on his soul*
That dyed on the rode!	*That died on the road*
For he was a good outlawe,	*For he was a good outlaw,*
And dyde pore men moch god.	*And did poor men much good.*

Extracts and translations from the 15th-century poem, *The Gest of Robyn Hode* showing Robin as a friend to the peasantry.

Given the long life that the legends of Robin Hood have had, must they be representative of real-life criminal activities during the medieval period? Or are they simply imaginative folk tales that have survived the years?

Real-life outlaws

During the first half of the 14th century, outlaw bands were causing serious problems and the levels of violence and public disorder were growing rapidly. In response to this the crown introduced a new form of commission, whose job it was to try and counteract this growth in crime. The fact that the royal treasury would benefit from all the fines the new commissions could impose may also have helped make this decision.

Despite this attempt to remove outlaw bands, from 1326 to 1346 a gang of outlaws, led by Eustace Folville, terrorised the Leicestershire countryside with little or no hindrance. In 1326, they began their criminal career.

Roger Bellers had been a baron of the exchequer and a nobleman of local standing. However, when called to answer for this crime Folville simply disappeared and his men could not be brought to trial and were declared outlaws. Rather than ending their activities, being outlawed seemed only to have increased them. They were eventually accused of five murders and a number of robberies, assaults, rapes and extortions. They even kidnapped and ransomed a justice of the King's bench!

How were these men able to commit such acts for such a long period of time without being punished?

Popular support

It seems that the Folvilles, despite their criminal activities, were popular with the local people of the area, who looked to them to even the score against what they saw as a corrupt and unfair judicial system. The Folville gang were in some sources seen as providing God's law and protecting local custom in the face of the law that came from the crown, rather than as law-breakers themselves.

SOURCE C

On 29 January, Master Roger Bellers was murdered in Leicestershire by one Eustace de Folville and his brothers, whom previously he had heaped with threats and injustices. This man had been an oppressor of his neighbours, both those in religious orders and others, on account of his greed for their possessions.

Extract from Henry of Knighton's 14th-century *Leicester Chronicle*.

SOURCE D

They wander in woods and other public and private places, ambushing wayfarers whom they rob and sometimes slay. In all these things they are aided and abetted by local people, who incite them to their evil deeds and shield them after they are done.

Historian E. L. G. Stones.

ACTIVITIES

1 What crimes did the Folvilles commit? Make a list of those that were similar and those that were different to those committed by Robin Hood and his men.

2 How similar is the story of the Folvilles to the legend of Robin Hood?

3 Does this mean that the stories of Robin Hood show us what medieval crime was actually like?

HISTORY DETECTIVE

Research the lives and crimes of these other medieval outlaws:

• Eustace the Monk

• Fulk fitzWarin

• Adam de Gurdon

How similar are their stories to the legend of Robin Hood? Do these findings change your view of what medieval crime was actually like?

2.6 Who was punished most harshly in the medieval period?

LEARNING OBJECTIVES

In this lesson you will:
- analyse change and continuity over time
- compare and contrast multiple factors.

People and the law

As the medieval period progressed the number of people charged with vagrancy increased. Vagrants were the homeless and it was widely believed that they were the cause of much crime and a real danger to society. Most of them begged in order to get money or food and this was seen as a real problem in the medieval world.

One of the key reasons for the change in treatment of beggars was the **Black Death**.

- The Black Death weakened the feudal system, meaning peasants were no longer tied to their home villages.
- Trade was growing and so was wealth.
- Towns started to expand and created new opportunities for jobs.
- Travel was now possible and people were more willing to move.

For some, these changes created new opportunities, but others could find no work and had to resort to crime.

KEY WORDS

Alms – charity payments made to help the very poor or sick, usually by wealthy people.

Black Death – a pandemic disease that spread across Europe from Asia in the mid-14th century. It is estimated that between 30 and 60 per cent of the population were killed.

SOURCE A

'If a man is such an animal that he has no knowledge of any trade and does not want to remain ignorant, he can take to begging until he knows... some trade...'

'Or if he cannot work because of a sickness he has, or because of old age...'

'Or if by chance he has become accustomed by his upbringing to live very delicately...'

'Or if he has the knowledge, the wish, and the ability to work, and is ready to work well, but does not immediately find someone who may want to give him work...'

'Or if he has the wages of his labour, but cannot live on them adequately on this earth...'

'Or if he wants to undertake some knightly deed to defend the faith...'

Extracts from *The Romance of the Rose*, 13th-century text, outlining who might be allowed to beg.

SOURCE B

Statute of Labourers, 1349 – 'no **alms** to be given to able-bodied beggars.

Statute of Cambridge (Poor Law), 1388 – those incapable of working should not move around the country and any beggar who is able-bodied should be severely punished.

Laws passed in the 14th century against vagabonds.

ACTIVITIES

Read Sources A and B.

1 How many of those allowed to beg in the 13th-century Source A would not be allowed once Source B became law?

2 Look at the effects of the Black Death. Why might Source B have been passed into law?

Barons and the law – part one

From the end of the 11th century there had been increasing friction between the king and the barons, mainly over where the rights of the king came from and what he could have personal control over, including local justice. By 1214 things had come to a head and a number of barons took up arms against the king. In 1215, King John was forced into signing the *Magna Carta*. This document included in it the idea of the rights of the freemen of England.

Barons and the law – part two

By the 1250s, trouble had flared up again between a group of barons and the king, now Henry III. Led by Simon de Montfort, Earl of Leicester, they complained of the high taxes the king was imposing and his refusal to listen to their advice. While compromise was reached in 1258, it could not last. By 1263 England was plunged into civil war, the barons versus the king. In 1265 the king's forces decisively defeated the barons at the battle of Evesham. Simon de Montfort was killed and the revolt was over.

By the late 14th and into the 15th centuries, the barons once again flexed their political muscles and, with their retainers acting as private armies, it led to an increasing number of disputes. The question was, could those using 'will and violence and force' be brought to justice?

VOICE YOUR OPINION!

You are King of England in 1250. You have just defeated a rebel baronial army and need to deal with the aftermath. Five senior noblemen have been captured and await your sentence, but they hold extensive lands and have many loyal men. How are you going to punish them?

You also need to deal with the ex-soldiers of the barons who are now roaming the land as vagabonds. It is a serious problem and needs dealing with. As King of England, how will you order them to be treated?

In both instances be prepared to back up your decision with evidence from the period.

Now imagine you are King of England in 1450. Would this make any difference to your decisions? If so, why?

SOURCE C

Law is always made by right; but will and violence and force are not right.'

An extract from *The Laws of Edward the Confessor*, a late 12th-century collection of laws and customs.

SOURCE D

After this [the battle of Evesham], a sentence of confiscation was pronounced at Westminster, against the king's enemies, whose lands the king bestowed without delay on his own faithful followers. But some of those against whom this sentence was pronounced redeemed their possessions by payment of a sum of money, others uniting in a body lay hid in the woods, living miserably on plunder.

An extract from *The Flowers of History*, a chronicle compiled in the early 13th century that explains what happened to some of the rebel barons.

SOURCE E

The sheriff informed us that he hath writing from the king that he shall make such a panel [jury] to acquit the Lord Moleyns and acquit his men.

An extract from a letter written in the 1450s by a servant of John Paston who was involved in a dispute over some of his property which Lord Moleyns' men had then attacked and taken over.

ACTIVITIES

3 How far do you think the sentiment in Source C was applied during the 13th century?

4 Using Sources C and D and the information on this page, make a list of who was following the law and who was using force during the 13th century.

5 Had this changed in any way by the time Source E was written?

2.7 How could we describe Early Modern Britain?

LEARNING OBJECTIVES

In this lesson you will:

- explore factors that changed Britain's social, economic and political landscape
- make a judgement about which factors contributed the most to this change.

GETTING STARTED

How could we describe Early Modern Britain?
A time of...

- brutal violence
- science and development
- social and economic turmoil?

The early modern period (1450–1750) has been described as the most brutally violent period in British history as it witnessed civil wars, conquest, rebellions, revolutions, massacres, assassinations, executions and even **regicide**. However, although Britain still was an agricultural society, it was also a time when Britain flourished during the Scientific Revolution and London was becoming a major centre for trade and commerce. The developments of this period affected crime in a number of different ways.

Between 1530 and 1630 the population increased from 2.5 million to 5 million people. There were not enough jobs to keep pace with the increase and this led to large numbers of unemployed people. Food production could not keep up with the huge increase in population.

KEY WORDS

Inflation – *an increase in the level of prices brought about by an increase in the amount of money in circulation.*

Regicide – *killing of a king.*

Socio-economic changes – *the relationship between the economy and people's lives.*

Factors that changed Britain

Inflation

The price of bread, which formed the greatest part of the diet of the poor, increased six fold between 1500 and 1600 while real wages increased less than half that amount. Rising **inflation** led to the creation of a mass of very poor people. On the other hand, these great **socio-economic changes** also created a community of rich farmers and brought enhanced profits for those with a surplus of grain to sell.

Economically diverse society

Because of socio-economic changes, many villages became divided between the poor on the one side, and a loose hierarchy of rich farmers, petty gentry and prosperous tradesmen on the other. They became the employers, the sources of credit and the overseers of the poor because of their influential positions as church wardens and constables.

Social and economic structure

In 1700, English communities numbered approximately 10,000 parishes and most of them were rural. Norwich, the second largest city, had 30,000 inhabitants and London had 500,000. By 1900 many towns and villages had become cities; for example, Liverpool's population rose from 22,000 in 1750 to 450,000 in 1900.

Conflict (civil war)

Conflict between Charles I and Parliament eventually led to a bloody civil war which divided the nation into two power blocks: Royalists fighting for King Charles and Parliamentarians fighting for Parliament. Life during the conflict was difficult and the effect was particularly felt in the villages as many farmers were forced to leave their families and farms to fight, which created severe financial and emotional strains on families. The aftermath of the English Civil War echoed for decades afterwards.

Monarchy and religion

The religion of the country depended on the religious views of the monarch. Therefore, disagreement with the monarch's religion was the same as treason and many paid the price as England in the 1600s experienced a sort of religious roller-coaster ride:

- Henry VIII separated the Church in England from the Roman Catholic Church in the 1530s.
- During the reign of his son, Edward VI (1547–53), England became more Protestant.
- From 1553 to 1558, England was ruled by Henry's daughter Mary I. She was determined to restore Roman Catholicism.
- When Elizabeth became queen in 1558 a new, Protestant, religious settlement was made.
- King James did not show great tolerance towards Catholics when he became king in 1603.

Treason, heresy and rebellion

A combination of factors, such as mounting religious and socio-economic uncertainties of the 1500s and 1600s created anxiety amongst the ruling elite and a series of protests and rebellions as well as an assassination attempt on James I's life merely increased these tensions.

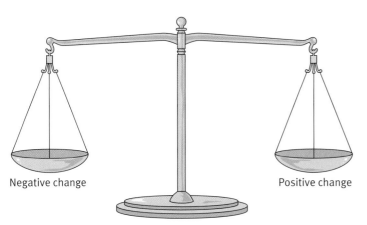

> ### ACTIVITY
>
> 1 On a sheet of paper, draw a set of scales similar to the big one on this page. Summarise each weight in turn, give it a weight that reflects how important you think it is and decide if it should go on the left or right hand side. At the end of the activity you should be able to discuss the main factors that changed Britain's social, economic and political landscape as well as make a judgement about which factors contributed the most to this change.

Negative change   Positive change

Religion was a serious business in the Early Modern Period. Changes to the official religion happened with almost every monarch and this meant that the people had to adapt as well. The result was that people were prosecuted for heresy when they failed to adapt their religion to match that of the monarch.

The trials were quite straightforward with defendants having a straight choice: renounce their ways and accept the new religion, or stick with their principles and suffer being burned at the stake. These executions were always public and held on busy days so that the majority of the population could see.

In Ipswich this end was given to seven people in this time period. All were accused of Protestantism and burned in the main town square during the reigns of Henry VIII and Queen Mary. A monument now stands in a local park to mark the event.

The Glorious Revolution

This was a series of events in 1688–89, which ended with the exile of James II and the accession to the throne of William and Mary. This event also brought a permanent change of power within the English constitution as it enabled Parliament to impose strict controls over future monarchs. The Glorious Revolution settled many of the political and religious problems as it led to the decision that future monarchs could only be Protestant and no other religion was allowed.

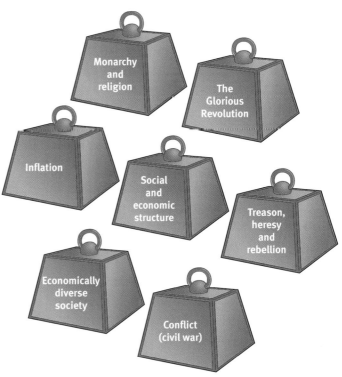

2.8 Why did the Tudors treat vagabonds so harshly?

LEARNING OBJECTIVES

In this lesson you will:

- investigate how vagabonds were treated under the Tudor monarchs
- reach a conclusion about how the treatment of vagabonds changed over time.

ACTIVITY

1 Create a living graph to examine the treatment of vagabonds in the Tudor period. Read the section on the treatment of vagabonds and decide whether their treatment became increasingly harsh or soft as the period progressed.

When you have completed the living graph, compare it with a partner's. How are the two graphs different? Why do you think this is?

Why did the number of poor people increase?

As we saw in the last lesson, the huge increase in population during the 16th century and the growing numbers of unemployed meant that many people were very poor. Even during stable economic periods there was still never enough work to go around. During the harvest, full-time work was available but only for short periods, so throughout slack periods of the agricultural year there would simply not be enough work to do. In bad times, those people who, at best, enjoyed a marginal existence would be thrown into acute poverty and sometimes even starvation.

There was no real social safety net to support the poor. This was left up to the local monasteries, the good will of ordinary individuals and the more affluent in society. The aftermath of the Wars of the Roses saw thousands of soldiers returning home to look for work, which rarely existed. They gained little from the fighting and returned carrying only their weapons. It is hardly surprising that some of them turned to robbery (see information about highway robbery on pages 70–3) or vagabondage. Many wealthy families, who before the war had given alms to the poor, had lost their wealth in the conflict, which made poverty worse as they were no longer able to support the poor. However, it was not the deserving poor, those who were incapable of earning a living, who were the problem.

To make matters even worse, large landowners changed the methods of farming from arable to sheep farming, which required only a fraction of the previous workforce – unemployment increased quickly. When Henry VIII closed down the monasteries in the 1530s, the relief poor people had received was suddenly taken away. Monks, nuns and other individuals who had been working in one of the 850 monasteries that were closed down, now became unemployed with low pensions. When inflation spiralled out of control at this time, most of them found themselves on the brink of extreme poverty.

Who were the vagabonds?

It was assumed that healthy looking men without obvious means of support were wilfully refusing to work and preferred to beg or indulge in crime. It was these '**sturdy beggars**' who were seen as the real problem. Most of them travelled alone between villages looking for work, but during particularly difficult times many vagrants travelled together in groups. These would be harvest workers, migrants, young people in search of apprenticeships, and to such individuals begging, stealing or working might well have been equally attractive methods of getting by. This group of mobile poor was seen as a threat to many people, particularly the ruling elite. Although a hardcore of sturdy beggars did exist, other people broke the law too.

How were vagabonds treated?

Tudor governments saw poverty as a cause of unrest: they dealt with the problem not for humanitarian reasons, but out of a belief that absolute poverty was a breeding ground for disorder, as indeed it often could be (see Chapter 4 on Protest). This fear of disorder lay behind most of the social legislation of the 16th century.

A series of poor harvests in the 1590s made it necessary to take more extreme measures against vagrants. The Poor Law of 1598 was divided into several sections:

Vagabonds were to be whipped, sent home and placed in houses of correction, and if they did not amend their ways, they were to be banished from the country. In 1601 the Great Poor Law Act was further improved and a system of dealing with the problems of poverty and vagrancy was set up which was infinitely more complex than anything dreamt of in 1500, for example, parishes had to collect poor rates to support workhouses and hospitals. Although the Elizabethan Poor Law did not cure the problems of poverty and vagrancy at a stroke, it was to last until 1834.

Fact file

Henry VIII 1509–47
Before the 1530s, most social legislation tended to lump several different categories of people together and treated poverty as a crime to be punished, rather than a social problem that could be improved. An act of 1531, however, distinguished between the **impotent poor** and the sturdy beggar, by giving licences to beg to the old, the sick and the disabled. No further provision was made for them, however, and the Act again failed to acknowledge that a man might wish to work but be unable to find employment. In fact, if any of these unemployed men and women were seen begging, or found to be vagrants, they would be 'tied to the end of a cart, naked, and be beaten with whips till his body be bloody…' J. Sharpe, *Crime in Early Modern England* (1999).

KEY WORDS

Impotent poor – *people too old or too sick to be able to work.*

Poor relief – *early local tax where money was raised to support the poor (particularly after the dissolution of the monasteries).*

Servitude – *forced labour.*

Sturdy beggars – *poor people who could work but refused and begged instead.*

Fact file

Edward VI 1547–53
Under the reign of Edward VI new laws to suppress vagrancy focused on using extreme punishments. Two years' **servitude** and branding with a 'V' was the penalty for a first offence, and attempts to run away were to be punished by lifelong slavery and, for a second time, execution. However, the Justices of the Peace, whose responsibility it was to enforce the new law, were reluctant to use such severe punishments. Consequently, the Act of 1550 revived the Act of 1531 which was less severe.

Fact file

Mary I 1553–58
There was no change of policy towards the treatment and punishment of vagrants under Queen Mary. The Act of 1531 was still carried out until her death in 1558.

Fact file

Elizabeth I 1558–1603
In 1563, Elizabeth took the first steps towards a compulsory rate for **poor relief**. Parishioners who refused to pay the rate could be imprisoned until a contribution had been made. If this seemed to be the beginning of actual reform to improve social conditions, then the Act of 1572 would prove otherwise: burning of the ear for the first offence, and persistent beggars would be executed. This measure did however identify that there were able-bodied men who were unemployed through no fault of their own. A more structured way of dealing with vagabonds started with the 1576 Act, which enforced the building of a house of correction to punish and employ persistent beggars. In 1593 the Act of 1572 was considered too severe so the 1531 Act was revived.

2.9 Who was a threat to the crown?

LEARNING OBJECTIVES

In this lesson you will:
- learn about rebellions and their causes
- analyse the reasons for rebellions and find links between them.

ACTIVITY

Read through the list of rebellions.

1 For each rebellion note down the following:
   - Who took part in the rebellion?
   - Who supported the rebellion?
   - What sparked the rebellion?

Throughout the 15th and 16th centuries there were numerous rebellions against the rule of the monarch. They varied in the threat they posed and the reasons behind them, but show that law and order were fragile throughout the period.

1497 – Perkin Warbeck

Perkin Warbeck landed in Cornwall aiming to take the throne from Henry VII by claiming to be the rightful heir. Despite aid from nobles in Burgundy, Scotland and Ireland, very few people joined his rebellion and it failed.

1536 – Lincolnshire Rising

Rumours were spread that new taxes were to be placed on bread, poultry and even marriages and burials. The people reacted angrily and with the help of the local gentry and clergy demanded greater representation. They were persuaded to disband after one week.

1536 – Pilgrimage of Grace

Led by a lawyer, over 30,000 people across Yorkshire eventually joined this peaceful protest against the dissolution of the monasteries and changes to the churches. They also had concerns over the loss of common land. Henry VIII heard their demands and issued a pardon to all but the leaders.

1549 – The Western Rebellion

The drive to make England fully Protestant and introduce a new prayer book led people from Cornwall and Devon into rebellion. Led by a local landowner and a priest they fought the local nobles until, after three months, they were beaten by the king's forces.

1549 – The Rebellions of Commonwealth

A series of uprisings occurred across 25 counties. It began when landowners enclosed common land, which led to numerous attacks on their property by the local people. It grew until 16,000 people, led by another local landowner, took control of Norwich and made demands about food prices, enclosure and religious practice. They were eventually defeated by the king's army near Yarmouth.

1554 – Wyatt's Rebellion

When it was announced that Queen Mary was to marry the Catholic King of Spain, Phillip, 300 Kentish men marched on London to demand she marry an Englishman. They were led by a rich landowner who hated Spain, but he won very few followers. He was quickly defeated by an army headed by leading noblemen.

1569 – Northern Rebellion

A rebellion by leading Catholic earls in northern England aimed at deposing the Protestant Queen Elizabeth I and replacing her with Mary, Queen of Scots. They took control of the north, east of the Pennines, and forced common people to join them. However, they received no aid from the north-west or Scotland and were defeated by the queen's army.

ACTIVITIES

2 Look at the reasons for each rebellion. Can you put the rebellions into groups that have similar reasons? What are these groups?
3 Which do you think was the most dangerous rebellion to the crown? Why?

The end of the Tudors

Queen Elizabeth I died on 24 March 1603 having reigned for 45 years. She never married and did not have any children to succeed her to the throne. Nor had she named a successor. Despite several other claimants to the throne, the crown was offered to, and accepted by, James VI, King of Scotland. He was crowned as James I of England on 25 July 1603.

Threats to the crown

Given the various threats that had faced James' Tudor predecessors, there would be reason for James to believe he might also face problems in his reign.

Foreign affairs

In 1603 England was at war with Spain and had been on-and-off since 1585. Spain was still a powerful country that proudly defended the Catholic faith and had access to the increasing wealth of the new colonies in the Americas. Just 40 years earlier the Spanish attempt at invasion had been foiled by the defeat of the Armada.

Religion – Catholicism

The increasing bitterness between Catholics and Protestants was a problem that continued across England. Now a Protestant country, the majority of people were suspicious of attempts to reinstate Catholicism as the one official religion. However there were still large numbers of Catholics living in England. Throughout the latter years of Elizabeth's reign, increasingly anti-Catholic laws had been passed that restricted or banned their worship. Numerous Catholic Jesuit priests were executed for their criticism of the Protestant state. James' mother, Mary, Queen of Scots, had been Catholic.

Religion – Puritanism

Within Protestantism itself, however, there were many divisions. The separatist ideas of Puritans, who refused to take part in Church of England services, also threatened the stability of the state. Puritans rejected any religious acts that were close to Catholicism and did not believe that kings were chosen by God and ruled by His right – an idea that James believed in very strongly.

Parliament

James now had to deal with the English Parliament, which had been increasing its rights and privileges during the final years of Elizabeth's reign. His relationship did not begin well as he argued with Parliament over the union of Scotland and England and also over the granting of money. James stated that he would not 'praise fools' and hoped that they would 'make use of your liberty with more modesty in time to come'.

ACTIVITIES

4 Make a list of the various threats to the crown in 1603.
5 How similar or different are these threats to those faced by the earlier Tudor monarchs?
6 If you were King James and could act to neutralise one of these threats, which would it be? Why?

2.10 How was the Gunpowder Plot reported?

LEARNING OBJECTIVES

In this lesson you will:
- look at the events of the Gunpowder Plot
- examine how different approaches affect sources.

Opening of Parliament

On 5 November 1605, James, King of England and Scotland, would start a new session of Parliament at the State Opening. Not only would the king himself be at Westminster, but so would the queen, members of the House of Lords and the House of Commons and numerous bishops. It was in fact a meeting of all the people who ran the country. For some this presented a target that was too good to pass up.

The events of the plot

Early 1603

On coming to the throne, James appoints a number of Catholics to important posts in the government and ends a number of religious fines imposed on Catholics.

Late 1603

James' government continue to enforce anti-Catholic laws and James himself speaks out against Catholics who put their loyalty to the Pope above that of their loyalty to their king.

Summer 1604

Plague comes to London and the State Opening is postponed until the next year.

May 1604

A group of influential Catholics meet to discuss the forming of a plot to overthrow the king and allow Catholicism to continue in England. It is led by Robert Catesby and included Sir Thomas Percy and Guy Fawkes amongst their number.

The plot was to hire a number of storerooms in the same building complex as the House of Lords, where the State Opening would be taking place. These storerooms would be filled with gunpowder that would be made to explode when the king was present. They would then lead a popular uprising from the Midlands that would place James' daughter, Elizabeth, on the throne as a Catholic queen.

Autumn 1604

Large quantities of gunpowder are purchased and stored at Catesby's house in Lambeth.

December 1604

Percy, using his position as a member of the king's bodyguard, is able to rent a storeroom directly underneath the House of Lords chamber where the gunpowder is hidden under a pile of fire wood.

May 1605

The conspirators, having hidden six barrels of gunpowder, leave London to avoid suspicion. Fawkes travels to Flanders until August while the final plans are made.

October 1605

Several conspirators become worried for the safety of other Catholics who would be killed if they went to the State Opening. One of the conspirators, possibly Francis Tresham, sends a letter warning his friend, Lord Monteagle not to attend.

Lord Monteagle hands the letter over to the authorities who are now aware that something is being planned.

5 November 1605

Guy Fawkes is taken to the Tower of London and tortured into revealing his fellow conspirators. King James himself orders that *'the gentler tortures are to be first used and thus by steps extended to greater ones'*.

4 November 1605

The vaults underneath the House of Lords are checked and Fawkes is discovered, along with 20 barrels of gunpowder. He has matches with him and admits to his plans. The plot is over.

1   Working in pairs, each of you should use the information on this page to write an account of the events of the Gunpowder Plot. You should include a background to the plot, what actually took place and what you think should be done to the captured conspirators.

One of you must choose to write from the point of view of Richard Rowlands, the other from the point of view of John Foxe. Read through the fact files below to establish their backgrounds and how you think that might affect their point of view.

Now compare your two accounts. In what ways are they different?

Fact file

Richard Rowlands was born in London in 1550 into an Anglo-Dutch family that had moved to England in the early 16th century. He attended university at Oxford but left without completing his degree, having converted to Catholicism while there.

He became involved in writing and publishing books, his first being a guidebook to England. However, his subject matter soon changed, and in 1581 he was forced to escape from arrest after secretly publishing a sympathetic account of the execution of the English Catholic priest, Edward Campion. He spent the next years travelling around Europe, writing about the attacks on Catholic priests in England, even at one stage living in Rome on a pension from the Pope.

In 1587, having settled in Antwerp, he published a book that was to become famous across Europe. It's title was *The Theatre of Cruelties of the Heretics of our Time*. It recounted the Protestant persecution of Catholics throughout Europe, but specifically those acts that took place in England.

He continued to be involved in the writing, printing and secret smuggling of pro-Catholic books into England. From his base in Flanders he also provided a vital connection between Catholic Jesuit priests, who were acting in secret in England, and their leaders on the Continent.

Fact file

Born in Lincolnshire in 1517, John Foxe was educated and then became a scholar at university in Oxford. In 1545 he resigned from his lecturing post due to his strong Protestant views, which were at odds with those of the Church of England, which he saw as too similar to Catholicism.

Foxe struggled to make ends meet until he became a tutor, and while in this position he was heavily involved in countering the rise of a cult to the Virgin Mary. By 1551 he had written and published his first pro-Protestant works. By 1554 Foxe had fled Queen Mary's new Catholic government in England, escaping to the Continent, where he began writing a history of persecuted Christians and acted as a preacher to Protestant English refugees in Frankfurt.

He continued to struggle to make a living in Europe until returning to, once-again Protestant ruled, England in 1559, where he was ordained as a priest. In this role he would make several well-known sermons in which he put forward his pro-Protestant views and attacked what he saw as the 'superstitious sect of popery'.

In 1563 Foxe finally published his major work, *Actes and Monuments of these Latter and Perillous Days, Touching Matters of the Church*, which quickly became known as *Foxe's Book of Martyrs*. It was a recounting of the persecutions of, mainly English, Protestants by Catholics. He would continue to revise this work in different editions up until the 1580s.

2.11 Should we burn effigies of Thomas Percy on 5 November every year?

LEARNING OBJECTIVES

In this lesson you will:

- find out about the Gunpowder Plot of 1605
- assess evidence and make conclusions from it.

GETTING STARTED

Hernando Cortez is considered a great explorer and the founder of Spanish colonies in South America. He conquered the Aztecs and became governor of the lands there. In Spain he is seen as one of their important historical figures, much like Christopher Columbus. However, some people have a different opinion. In 1975 the singer Neil Young released a song called 'Cortez the Killer' where he offers a different interpretation. Compare the verses below about Cortez and the Aztec leader Montezuma:

Cortez:
He came dancing across the water
With his galleons and guns
Looking for the new world
In that palace in the sun.

He came dancing across the water
Cortez, Cortez
What a killer.

Montezuma:
Hate was just a legend
And war was never known
The people worked together
And they lifted many stones.

They carried them to the flatlands
And they died along the way
But they built up with their bare hands
What we still can't do today.

How can such different views exist of the same event?

In this lesson you are going to look at the figure of Thomas Percy and his role in the gunpowder plot. He is not the most well known of the conspirators who tried to kill the King in 1605, but he did play a role. Guy Fawkes is the name that everyone knows, and after all, he was caught in the cellars ready to light the gunpowder. He was killed and became a legend for his action, but should we remember others for their role too? The information about Thomas Percy is split into rounds and for each one you need to assess whether you think he deserves to be burned on the bonfires every year.

ACTIVITY

1 Play historical hangman. Read the information below and for every point that you feel is important enough to make Percy a burning effigy, mark down one line. In total you will need ten lines to hang him: four for the frame and noose and six for the body.

Round one – background

- Percy was given the job of constable of Alnwick Castle by a relative. He was unpopular with the locals because he was strict and ruthless.
- In 1596 he was briefly imprisoned for killing a horse stealer in a border skirmish. He shot the man in the back without warning.
- His own records show that in 1602 '… there was a bell carryed out of *Warkworth castle* and sold by Sir John Ladyman, Mr Percye's deputie, to a Scottishman for £10, and a token sent by Mr Percye to one Henrye Finch to carrye the bell to the Scottishman's ship at Alnmouth'.
- Also he was accused of bribery, 'John Wilkinson of Over Busdon says that Mr Percy had £30 for his farmhold, being but 18s. of ancient rent, besides £4 he gave to Sir John Ladyman and Gabriel Ogle for procuring the bargain at Mr Percy's hands'.

Round two – religion

- Percy was born and raised a Protestant.
- He converted to Catholicism before 1591, when he married into a Catholic family.
- He helped the Earl of Northumberland petition the King of Scotland for understanding towards the Catholic faith. They thought they had succeeded, but when James also became King of England, he made no changes and refused to repeal the legislation against them.

Round three – the plot

- In May 1604, Robert Catesby gathered supporters together and explained a plan to kill King James and most MPs. Thomas Percy was there with Guy Fawkes and two others.

- Later, others were added to the plot.
- The first idea was to tunnel under Parliament from a building nearby. However, Percy managed to hire a cellar under the House of Lords. The cellar was filled with gunpowder by the group.
- Guy Fawkes would be given the job of lighting the fuse. He had been recruited because he had expertise in this area so he was given the task of creating the explosion.

Round four – discovery
- One of the plotters was worried that the explosion would kill his relative, *Lord Monteagle*. On 26 October, Tresham sent Lord Monteagle a letter warning him not to attend Parliament on 5 November.
- Monteagle informed the authorities that something was wrong and the King's Chief Minister had the cellars searched. Guy Fawkes was caught and arrested. Percy was quickly uncovered as part of the Catholic plot – the cellar was rented to him.

Round five – the chase
- The government quickly released a proclamation for Percy's arrest.

Round six – death
- Four of the conspirators left London and went to Staffordshire. The Sheriff of Worcester was informed of their hiding place after reports came to him about breaking into barns and horse stealing. On 8 November the house was surrounded by troops, the men tried to surrender, but the Sheriff refused and stormed the house. Within minutes, Robert Catesby, Thomas Percy, Christopher Wright and John Wright were killed.

SOURCE A

Artist's impression of the plotters – Percy is the fourth from the right, waving a finger.

ACTIVITY

2 In groups of three:
  - Identify key themes/factors amongst the clues.
  - What clues link together?
  - Why do you think that the King acted so swiftly and strongly against the plot?
  - Can you think of modern examples where governments have had to act quickly to deal with protests and threats?

SOURCE B

My lord, out of the love I have for some of your friends, I want to make sure you are safe. Because of this I would advise you to not attend this sitting of parliament because God and man have agreed to punish the wickedness of this time. Do not think this is a joke, go to your estate in the country where you will be safe, because although there is no sign of any problem yet, this parliament will receive a terrible blow, but they will not see who it is that hurts them. This advice should not be ignored as it may do you some good, and it can do you no harm because the danger will have passed as soon as you have burned this letter. I hope God grants you the grace to make good use of it, and that he protects you.

Letter from Tresham to Monteagle.

SOURCE C

Whereas one Thomas Percy, a bodyguard to the King is found to have been involved in one of the most horrible acts of Treason ever planned, that is, while the King, Queen, Prince, all the nobility and the commons were in the upper house, it was to be blown up with gunpowder (and for this purpose a great deal of powder was moved into a cellar under the house which was found there this morning), and Percy has now run away.

These commands call our Officers and loyal subjects to willingly search for Percy and arrest him using all possible means, but keeping him alive, so we can discover the rest of the plotters. Percy is a tall man with a great broad beard and a good face. His beard and head is sprinkled with white hairs, however his head is whiter than his beard. He stoops slightly and has a good colour in his face as well as big feet and short legs.

Proclamation for the arrest of Percy.

2.12 Why were women hanged from oak trees in 1645?

LEARNING OBJECTIVES

In this lesson you will:

- demonstrate an understanding of why witchcraft started
- explain what factors were involved in the start of witchcraft.

By contrast to Europe, where, for example, 900 women were reported to have been burnt at the stake in Lorraine between 1580 and 1595, or the 1000 women at Come in 1524, fewer women were tried and executed for witchcraft in England. In fact, far more people were hanged for stealing a sheep or a purse than for witchcraft. The witchcraft craze started in Switzerland in the 13th century, peaked in England in the 1640s and popular belief in witches survived well into the 19th century. Now let us consider what contributed to the spread of belief in witchcraft.

In 1941 the battleship HMS Hood was sunk off Greenland killing all but three of its 1418 crew. Before the incident had become publicly known, a **medium** named Helen Duncan described the disaster during a séance. This soon reached the ears of the security services. Helen Duncan's work was investigated until January 1944 when she was arrested. Two months later, she was convicted at the Old Bailey and sentenced to nine months' imprisonment for conspiracy to break the Witchcraft Act of 1735. This act had been passed to destroy belief in witches and its intended use was to fine or imprison people who claimed to have the powers of a witch.

Helen Duncan was eventually released after much campaigning – even the Prime Minister Winston Churchill wrote to the Home Secretary branding the charge as '... obsolete tomfoolery'. She was released from prison on 22 September 1944.

KEY WORDS

Familiar – *in early-modern British superstition, familiars, or imps, were animal-shaped spirits that served witches and demons. They supposedly served as their owners' domestic pets and servants, but also helped bewitch enemies.*

Medium – *person who acts as a link between the living and the spiritual world of the dead.*

SOURCE A

Helen Duncan – one of Britain's last witches?

In July 1944 another medium, Jane Rebecca York, was found guilty on seven counts against the Witchcraft Act of 1735. She was fined £5 and placed on good behaviour for three years if she promised to hold no more séances. The light sentence was due to her age of 72.

Witchcraft, by any definition, was decriminalised in England in 1951, after more than 400 years.

ACTIVITIES

1 Examine Helen Duncan's story.

   a What can you learn about attitudes to mediums in the 20th century?

   b Why do you think Helen Duncan was treated so harshly in 1944?

Where did accusations about witchcraft mainly appear?

Generally, the accusation of witchcraft was usually the outcome of a series of incidents and growing tensions whereby a number of villagers would become increasingly suspicious of one of their fellow villagers, normally a woman. For example, Margaret Harkett was caught picking peas from a neighbour's field and when asked to return them, she threw them down with an angry curse after which no peas grew on the neighbour's field. Margaret was executed at Tyburn in 1585 for witchcraft.

As far as England was concerned there is no real evidence to suggest the existence of anything like an organised witch cult with covens, black sabbaths or aerial transportation (although a broomstick is mentioned in one trial). The women who were unlucky enough to be accused of being witches tended to be the most vulnerable members of a small community: childless, lonely old widows on the brink of poverty, more often than not reduced to begging from their neighbours.

The English Civil War increased the number of this socio-economic group. Often, these unfortunate women's only companion was a pet toad, weasel or cat. These animals transformed in the imagination of their accusers into **familiars** given to them by the devil to perform acts of evil. If these women happened to have a distinguishing mark such as a devil's teat under the armpit, a hump back or hair on the chin, suspicion became certainty. Once an accusation had been made a familiar or a distinguishing mark was easy to find – Matthew Hopkins, the Witchfinder General (see pages 64–5) only needed to see a tiny fly settling on the victim's shoulder to be certain that it was a witch's familiar.

(see pages 64–5)

2 Why did accusations about witchcraft occur in the 17th century?

3 What 'evidence' did people find that linked some women to witchcraft?

4 Create a flow-chart showing how these accusations could happen.

HISTORY DETECTIVE

You have come across an old diary belonging to a local magistrate in King's Lynn, Norfolk. It is dated 1645. Many of the pages are illegible but some are still clear enough to understand.

Examine the scraps from the book below and in groups of three, answer this question:

Why were women hanged from oak trees in 1645?

Village communities began to grow where some became very rich and some very poor.

A witch would let animals drink their blood.

Nearly everyone in the village got married, it was expected.

Matthew Hopkins called himself the Witchfinder General.

It was believed that witches could control animals such as cats and goats.

There was little understanding of disease in the 17th century.

Constant changes in religion had made people sceptical about their faith.

Symptoms of illness were often mistaken for the work of the devil.

Women who lost their husbands, e.g. during the civil war, often had to beg to survive.

Prices were rising faster than wages and a bad harvest could mean disaster.

Elderly widows stood out as they did not have a family.

The English Civil War (1624–49) had left a vast power gap in England.

There was no real social network in the 1600s to aid the poor.

In the 1640s Matthew Hopkins travelled East Anglia for witches.

King James I wrote a book about witchcraft called Daemonology.

Whatever people could not explain was put down to the devil or spirits.

Oliver Cromwell created the New Model Army during the Civil War.

People were very suspicious when their animals died suddenly.

Women could not defend themselves in court; men had to speak for them.

People felt guilty when they did not give money or food to the poor.

Belief in magic and witchcraft had always been part of village life.

2.13 Case study: Was Matthew Hopkins simply a product of his time?

LEARNING OBJECTIVES

In this lesson you will:

- explore the role of an individual in worsening attitudes towards the persecution of women as witches

- make a judgement about how far Matthew Hopkins was a product of the time period.

GETTING STARTED

Examine Sources A and B.

a What similarities/differences can you find between the history of the witch-hunting craze in England and the message in the sources?

b How far is the language of Sources A and B reminiscent of the persecution of witches in Britain during the 16th and 17th centuries?

While, by 1640, ordinary people may still have believed in witchcraft, it was no longer an important issue for the government, the courts or theological debate. However, during the Civil War, particularly in the year 1642, the issue of witchcraft resurfaced. The years 1644–45 saw the most dramatic witch-hunting episode in eastern England when prejudices such as **misogyny** became more pronounced and widespread.

Matthew Hopkins, a gentleman living at Manningtree, Essex, became concerned about what he regarded as the local frequency of witches. His worry struck a responsive chord with the community, which culminated in the prosecution of 36 women, of whom half were executed at Chelmsford in 1645. Hopkins received a 20 shilling (£1) fee for each person found guilty of witchcraft by local magistrates.

KEY WORDS

Misogyny – *hatred of women.*

SOURCE B

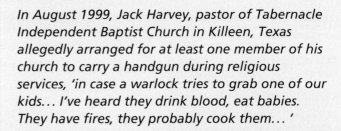

In August 1999, Jack Harvey, pastor of Tabernacle Independent Baptist Church in Killeen, Texas allegedly arranged for at least one member of his church to carry a handgun during religious services, 'in case a warlock tries to grab one of our kids... I've heard they drink blood, eat babies. They have fires, they probably cook them... '

Extract from an article published in the *Fort Worth Star-Telegram* in Texas, USA, about hatred against Wiccas (people who practise Wicca, a pagan religion started in 1954), 1999.

SOURCE A

The suspicion under which the Jews are held is murder. They are charged with enticing Gentile children and Gentile adults, butchering them, and draining their blood. They are charged with mixing this blood into their mass's unleavened bread and using it to practise superstitious magic. They are charged with torturing their victims, especially the children, and during this torture they shout threats, curses, and cast spells against the Gentiles...

Julius Streicher, editorial in *Der Stuermer*, newspaper of the German Nazi Party, 1934.

SOURCE C

[Hopkins is being questioned about whether he becomes rich from finding witches]

'... judge how he [Hopkins]... enriches himself by considering the vast sum of money he takes from every town, he takes 20 shilling per town, and must sometimes ride 20 miles for that... and may find 3 or 4 witches or just one, cheap enough, and this is what he takes to maintain his company with 3 horses.'

Matthew Hopkins, *The Discovery of Witches*, Query 14.

This amount may not seem like a lot of money, but in those days it was a small fortune particularly when the average weekly wage was approximately 2½p! Not surprisingly, Hopkins found quite a few witches in the area. This brief yet horrifying episode witnessed the trials of around 250 people, of whom 100 were executed.

During this time accusations of witchcraft had spread into Suffolk, which would have one of the highest number of executions. There were also trials and hangings in Norfolk and Huntingdonshire and elsewhere in East Anglia.

The majority of the people tried and executed during the Hopkins witch-hunts were poor, elderly women on the edge of ordinary society. The difference between this period and earlier witch-hunts was the widespread presence of the devil in the accused women's confessions, with details of the pact and accounts of sexual intercourse between the witch and the devil – features that were uncommon in the vast majority of trials before the 1640s. The most logical explanation to this new phenomenon could be credited to the interrogation techniques carried out by Matthew Hopkins and his companion John Stearne.

In Manningtree, and in thousands of places around the country, differences in religious beliefs, attitudes towards work as well as divisions caused by extreme poverty all ran deep. These were all made worse by the upheavals and pressures generated by civil war. Matthew Hopkins was not so much the general of the witchfinding movement but more an assistant who helped things along. It took a lot of people to hang a witch: witnesses, constables, midwives, magistrates, gaolers, clerks, judges, jurors, sheriffs, executioners, neighbours, and gravediggers – the list is endless. Witch-hunters gave people confidence to act and people like Matthew Hopkins provided his expertise, but not more than that.

Matthew Hopkins and John Stearne remained unrepentant about their actions.

SOURCE D

'... let no man doubt but that the finding out of such miscreants (criminals) is an acceptable service before God' [and on the subject of torturing women to confess he explains that] '... they had better provisions, either meat or drink, than at their own houses.'

John Stearne, *A Confirmation and Discovery of Witchcraft*, 1648.

Fact file

Some sources claim that Parliament employed Matthew Hopkins to undertake his duties. In fact, Hopkins appointed himself Witchfinder General and used the disorder of the Civil War to his advantage, allowing him to run roughshod over East Anglia without being confronted by any law and order.

Despite the legend that Matthew Hopkins was tried and executed as a witch, he in fact died of tuberculosis in 1647 and his fellow witch-hunter John Stearne disappeared into obscurity soon afterwards. Nevertheless, Hopkins' actions created widespread panic and terror in a population already terrified by a bloody Civil War.

VOICE YOUR OPINION!

'The people who persecute asylum seekers and travellers are the modern heirs to the witchfinders of the past.'
Do you agree with this? Remember to give your reasons.

ACTIVITIES

The role of Matthew Hopkins in intensifying the persecution of witches in the 1640s has been fiercely debated amongst historians. For example, many have considered whether Matthew Hopkins was simply a product of the period.

1 Work in pairs or groups of three. Begin by writing down all your ideas about this question on some sticky-notes, cards or scraps of paper. For example, think about major events of the time period and who the key individuals were.

2 Group your ideas according to the factors below (or your own factors). Do you all agree?
   • Monarchy • Religion • Conflict • Economy

3 Now create an ideas map with the sticky-notes, with the factors as main bubbles, the key question in the middle and your key points flying out from each factor bubble. Be prepared to explain your map to the rest of the class. You may wish to write a brief explanation to your ideas map.

4 When you have established the main reasons that support your argument, write a summary to this question:
   Would Matthew Hopkins have been as vicious and violent in any other period? Explain your reasons.

2.14 How did attitudes towards witchcraft change over time?

LEARNING OBJECTIVES

In this lesson you will:

- analyse different factors which influenced why people believed in witchcraft
- identify trends in how attitudes to witchcraft changed over time.

GETTING STARTED

Examine Source A.

a What can you learn about the attitudes to witchcraft?

b Was fear of witches the only motive for dealing with these individuals so harshly?

In 1644 the crime of witchcraft was a century old in England and people's beliefs about witches had dramatically changed from hysteria to calm and then back again.

Elizabeth I (1558–1603)

When Elizabeth became queen in 1558, exiled senior Protestant clerics returned from Europe filled with concerns about the dangers of sorcery. In fact, by the early 1560s, the Protestant corners of England were no longer hearing rumours of magic but cases of full-blown witchcraft. Consequently, The Witchcraft Act was published in 1563 and it carried the death penalty. The first execution occurred a year later in Essex. Elizabethan thinking had raised the status of witchcraft from a part of the suspicion of rural life into the ultimate spiritual crime.

James I (1603–25)

When James I came to the throne in 1603 he immediately changed the Witchcraft Act so that all cases of witchcraft were to be dealt with by the courts. James was infamous for embracing a popular issue of the time and developing an 'expert' knowledge of it. Before 1590, few academics, religious scholars or lawyers had shown any real interest in the idea of witchcraft and therefore to James it was not a trendy topic. However, by the early 1600s James I had become so devoted to the cause that he even interrogated women about witchcraft by himself. He also wrote a book – *Daemonology*. According to James, witches were vermin that had to be exterminated as they switched their allegiance from God to the Devil.

SOURCE A

1590: The trial of the North Berwick Witches. This trial involved several people who were convicted of having used witchcraft to create a storm in an attempt to sink the ship on which King James VI of Scotland and Anne of Denmark had been travelling.

Daemonology was not only an academic discussion in favour of persecuting witches, but also a practical manual for the job. Strangely enough, when the book was republished for the second time in 1616, King James was more interested in deer-hunting than witchcraft. He even scolded a couple of judges for executing nine women for the crime of witchcraft at Leicester; this had a significant impact on people who had political or any other ambitions as they all wanted to please their king – executions decreased.

Not overnight

Historian Hugh Thomas states that witchcraft trials began to decline after 1701. However, although the educated elite accepted new scientific discoveries as evidence that the world had changed, it took longer amongst the rural population where the notion of magic and belief in witchcraft was ingrained in everyday life.

ACTIVITY

1   Using the information in this lesson create a living graph that demonstrates when people's attitudes changed and what event or individual made them change and why.

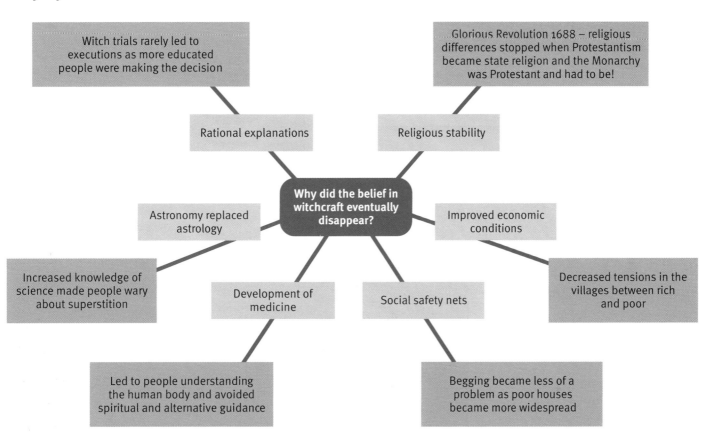

ACTIVITIES

2   In pairs create your own copies of the concept map above. All the notes around the enquiry question – **Why did the belief in witchcraft eventually disappear?** – are supporting pieces of information that will help you to answer that question.

Identify and colour code those notes that are:
*   most important
*   slightly important
*   not important.

3   You have recently been employed by The History Channel and as your first assignment you have been asked to produce a five-minute documentary with the controversial title 'The Witch-Hunting Craze: The Bloodbath of the Innocents'. Using video-editing software or an A3 storyboard, plan and create the whole documentary including the following factors.

*   Background to the time period. For example: why people believed in witches, religious issues and changes in monarchy.
*   Will you involve other people in the programme: for example, historians, politicians, authors, religious spokespeople including both Catholics and Protestants?
*   What events and individuals encouraged the persecution of witches?
*   Why did the witch-hunting craze eventually disappear?
*   Conclude the trailer with your final thoughts on the topic.

Use pages 62–67 to research and complete your assignment.

2.15 How did the government deal with 'social crimes'?

LEARNING OBJECTIVES

In this lesson you will:
- be able to select relevant information
- categorise information into key factors.

KEY WORDS

Capital offence – *a crime that was punished by hanging.*

Game – *any animal hunted for food and not domesticated, for example, deer.*

Poaching – *illegal fishing and hunting.*

Social crime – *a crime that people generally do not regard as a proper crime.*

GETTING STARTED

Study Sources A and B. Compare these two sources as evidence of sympathy for smugglers.

SOURCE A

*If you wake at midnight, and
    hear a horse's feet,
Don't go drawing back the
    blind, or looking in the
    street,
Them that asks no questions
    isn't told a lie.
Watch the wall, my darling,
    while the Gentlemen go by!*

*Five-and-twenty ponies,
Trotting through the dark –
    Brandy for the Parson,
'Baccy for the Clerk;
Laces for a lady; letters for a
    spy
And watch the wall, my
    darling, while the
    Gentlemen go by!*

From *The Smugglers Song*, by Rudyard Kipling.

SOURCE B

Illustration from *Smuggling in the British Isles*, 2007.

1. Use the statements below to complete tasks **a** and **b**.

   a How far was the government responsible for creating the problems of **poaching** and smuggling?

   - Group the statements into categories, for example, 'political', 'social', 'economy', 'law and order' or add other ones you feel would be appropriate.
   - Choose 12 statements that best help to answer the question.
   - Which statements are the most important in answering the question? Rank them according to their importance.

   b Was it only the government that regarded smuggling as a serious crime in the 18th century?

   - Choose 12 statements that best help to answer the question.
   - Which statements are the most important in answering the question? Rank them according to their importance.

1. The rich and powerful had a lot to lose and felt that some types of people were a threat to them.

2. In 1723 the 'Black Act' made poaching with a blackened face a **capital offence**. Possessing poaching equipment could mean a year in prison or transportation.

3. Many ordinary people approved of smuggling, or took part in it.

4. The government believed smuggling to be serious crime that damaged the country's economy severely.

5. The law against poaching meant that farmers could not kill animals that ate their corn, or use animals such as rabbits and pheasants to feed their own families.

6. Smugglers were generally seen as harmless individuals who were on the public's side as they ensured that prices were kept low on goods taxed by an unreasonable government.

7. Some people left their barns or cellars unlocked and did not ask questions about what was put in there.

8. Even respectable people were involved, sometimes for money, sometimes because they did not regard smuggling as a crime.

9. Threat of violence sometimes kept local magistrates from convicting smugglers, while juries selected from local villages were either too scared to act or supported the smugglers.

10. The vast majority of MPs and other rulers of the country were generally landowners.

11. The government collected much of its income from customs duties – tax paid on the import of goods such as tea, cloth, wine and spirits. The tax was high, for example up to 130% for tea, so these items became expensive.

12. No effective police force existed in the period from 1600 to the 1750s.

13. The **Game** Act of 1671 made it illegal to hunt certain animals. Ordinary people could not even shoot a pigeon that landed on their property. People who owned large tracts of land could hunt anywhere without getting punished.

14. Several economists blamed the government for the rise in smuggling and said that they were 'pushing people into crime'.

15. Many people in England became richer in the 17th and 18th centuries, but the majority remained very poor – especially when bad harvests increased food prices or a fall in trade meant that people lost jobs.

16. Smuggling and poaching have been regarded as '**social crimes**' as people did not regard them as crimes. Social crimes still exist today with the advent of music and movie downloads.

17. Prime Minister William Pitt lowered duties on certain items, such as tea from 130% to 12.5% in the 1780s, so smuggling became less profitable. Further reductions of duties in the 1800s put an end to the kind of smuggling that went on so openly in the 1700s.

18. For the poor, wild animals were an important source of food.

19. Some poachers were taking game on quite a large scale, to sell to merchants.

20. Wherever governments try to stop, or tax, the flow of goods that people desire, smugglers work.

21. Smugglers used violence and sometimes killed for their goods. The Hawkthurst Gang, an infamous group of smugglers, once tortured a man to death for stealing two bags of tea.

22. Hard drugs such as heroin and cocaine are key products for smugglers today.

2.16 Get your sources sorted!

The highwayman: A gentleman robber or violent thug?

In this lesson you will:
- explore different interpretations of highwaymen
- use evidence to support your own judgement.

1 Study Sources A–F. 'The highwayman: a gentleman robber or violent thug?' How far do the sources support either view? Use the sources and your knowledge to explain your answer.

The traditional highwayman is a masked, caped, tricorn-hatted gentleman astride a beautiful horse, pistol ready whilst calling out the memorable commands 'Stand and Deliver!' His victims are travellers with too much money for their own good. Luckily, the highway robber will share this unnecessary wealth with the poor and needy. This representation is far from the reality of highwaymen.

Answering an interpretation question

This exercise will help you to plan out and write a top-level answer for an interpretation question.

How to answer an interpretation question

Step 1

Read the question and underline what it is asking you to do. What do you know already? Annotate your thoughts about why he might be considered a gentleman robber or a thug. What do you think? Make sure that you have an argument.

Step 2

Make sure you examine both sides of the argument carefully dealing with one issue at a time. Use all the sources (if the question asks you to) in your writing

without referring to each one separately. Instead organise them into 'sets', for example, Source A might agree about a particular issue, whereas Sources D and H disagree; Sources B and C might be discussing a similar issue and so on. For example:

'Both Sources B and D support the claim that the highwayman was a gentleman, particularly Source D which informs us that Duval even danced with the lady, a true sign of a perfect gentleman.'

Step 3

Be critical of the source material. For example there might be some sources that support one of the claims but you might not consider it to be reliable. Explain why. For example:

'Although there is evidence to suggest that some highwaymen did indeed live up to this reputation, as Maclain explains in Source C when he returns the money taken, most of these men were of 'very unlikable character' as suggested by Source E . Therefore, the idea that some were dancing with their frightened victims is not true and probably only forms part of romantic writers of the time like in Source D.'

Step 4

Make a judgement and use your own knowledge to support your writing. For example:

'The highwayman could be seen as a gentleman by some people, but the chance of meeting a friendly highway robber on Hampstead Heath in the middle of the night is rather unlikely. It also seems likely that many victims who wrote about their experiences did so for reasons of financial or social gain like Sources B and D which all explain a rather positive encounter. However, most actual robberies were done by men who sought fast money without caring much for those lives they ruined 'who may have worked hard for what little they had', which helps to explain that most victims were not very well off at all.'

SOURCE A

1860 painting by William Powell Frith entitled *Claude Duval*.

... the Hours of 10 &11 the said night, attacked, in a place above a mile beyond Longford leading to Hounslow Heath, by a little siz'd man, who had on a light drab coloured horseman's coat, the cape buttoned about his face and his hat flapped before, his horse of a dark bay colour, with a switch tail, who immediately presented a pistol to my breast, and bid me to stand and deliver my money... and immediately put his hand into my pocket (the pistol being still at my breast) and took thereout between 13 & 14 shillings being all I had about me, after which he said I must go along with him, and then he took my horse by the head, with his pistol in his hand, and led him up a Lane that was just by, and thereunder a hedge he dismounted his horse and searched my pockets, boots... and after having kept me about 20 minutes, mounted his horse, asked me if I knew him (but commanded me at the same time not to look in his face) and what was my name, and then rode off, without taking my dispatches... or anything else except my money. The highway man at going off shook me by the hand, and said, that provided I would not tell that I had been stopp'd & robbed, whenever I came that way again, if I should meet him, I need only tell him my name, and he would not stop me any more.

An account from Nathan Carrington, of the king's messengers, about being robbed at night on the highway, National Archives.

SOURCE **C**

Obliged a couple of sneaking **footpads** to refund the week's wages they had taken from a poor labourer.

From James Maclain's letter to *The Public Advertiser*, 29 February 1764.

SOURCE **D**

Most highway robberies were prosecuted by men of low status and on foot. The total number of robberies was small and the value of goods stolen was not great. One group of highwaymen, led by Patrick O'Bryan, robbed a house in Wiltshire during which they tied up three servants, the owner and his wife, gang raped his daughter and finally set the building on fire, with fatal results for the three servants. Violence is a theme that is rarely absent from the highwaymen's biographies.

J. Sharpe, *Dick Turpin*, 2005.

SOURCE **E**

... His purpose in life was to fill his belly and acquire enough money to enjoy the good life whoring, gambling and drinking... and to do so at the expense of others who may have worked hard for what little they had. In reality the highwayman was a very unlikable character.

D. Brandon, *Stand and Deliver – a History of Highway Robbery*, 2004.

SOURCE **F**

Walpole, a well known author, recorded his experience of being robbed by the infamous highwaymen Plunkett and Maclaine in Hyde Park, London. Walpole wrote that Maclaine's pistol 'went off accidentally and razed the skin under my eye... ' The next morning he receives a letter from Maclaine offering his apologies for any inconvenience caused. Walpole stated that his brief relationship with the highway robber was carried out 'with the greatest good breeding on both sides'.

Extract from *Supplement to the Letters of Horace Walpole*.

KEY WORDS

Footpad – *robber on foot.*

GradeStudio

Examiner's tips

The interpretation question tends to be at the end of the exam and will undoubtedly involve the most marks, so it is crucial you take time answering it. It will require you to assess whether the highwayman was indeed a gentleman robber or a simple thug. Not all views of highwaymen are the same. Some writers confirm one another while others contradict.

2.17 Why did highway robbery increase?

LEARNING OBJECTIVES

In this lesson you will:

- demonstrate why highway robbery existed
- identify reasons why highway robbery disappeared.

In the popular video game *Grand Theft Auto*, one of the main activities is hijacking cars.

A weekend crackdown on begging in London has been branded 'totally inappropriate' by a leading homelessness charity, Crisis. The policy of taking the DNA and fingerprints of beggars in Westminster began last night. Crisis said it will 'criminalise some of society's most vulnerable people… and grossly demeaning to homeless people.' Westminster is thought to have about 300 beggars. Police officers will arrest beggars spotted by council teams and take fingerprints and a DNA sample. The council said in a statement: 'Beggars identified as repeat offenders or those that are active around cash points will be considered for post conviction ASBOs [anti-social behaviour orders] if their behaviour continues.' Crisis said: 'Begging…[is] a stark sign of social deprivation, and unless this is recognised the problem will not be solved.'

Extract from the *Guardian* newspaper, February 2004.

GETTING STARTED

Carjacking is where a driver is forced to hand over their car to attackers and, in the most extreme cases, is threatened at gunpoint. The police believe carjacking is a response to advances in vehicle security. Thieves are avoiding trying to break into locked cars in favour of trying to get car keys. In 2002, Britain experienced a 'carjacking crisis' where several cases of car hijacking occurred – people were given tips on what to do if they believed the crime was being committed. In 2004, Scotland Yard stated that carjacking was 'affecting the whole of the country' and was a matter of real public concern.

1 Consider Sources A and B. Are they linked in some way?

2 How far do you think a video game or film can influence public perception about certain crimes?

3 What questions does the existence of this crime bring up?

Why did highway robbery exist?

Robbery that took place on or near the king's highway (including on the streets of London as they were designated highways by one of the Transportation Acts) was classed as highway robbery and was a common crime between 1450 and 1750. Many people who committed highway robbery were executed. This was because the combination of violence and theft with obstructing the freedom to travel, made these some of the most serious offences dealt with by the courts. During the Elizabethan period the government, for the first time, expressed concerns about gangs of mounted robbers operating on the outskirts of London. By the early 1700s, the frequency of highway robbery, similar to street crime today, came to provide people's opinion at the time with an indicator for the general state of law and order.

ACTIVITY

1 Why did highway robbery increase? In groups of two or three, examine the nine cards giving reasons why this happened. Copy them onto a sheet of paper, cut them out and place them in order of importance in a diamond shape (like in the example) with the most important reason at the top and the least at the bottom of the diamond. Discuss.

VOICE YOUR OPINION!

Look back at Source A. How far do you think video games or films can contribute to the increase of certain crimes?

Some highway robbers were highly organised and had 'spies' in taverns, like landlords, who were watching to see who was worth holding up on the road.

Because there were few banks people tended to carry money and jewellery around with them.

There was no organised or effective police force.

After serious conflicts such as the Thirty Year's War, Wars of the Roses, Civil War and the Napoleonic Wars, demobilised soldiers returned home to find themselves without work. Some of them turned to crime.

There were many lonely areas of heathland or woodland near towns and, in particular London, for example Hounslow Heath.

Britain was a rural country, with very few large towns. Roads were primitive so travel was slow and there were few travellers. Therefore, roads were quiet with lots of isolated country places.

The Civil War witnessed the development of more sophisticated weapons and guns became easier to get hold of and cheaper to buy.

A lot of literature in the 1600s popularised the image of the *Gentleman Robber*.

Many people resented the wealthy landowning classes, their rulers, and admired highway robbers as they symbolised the fight against inequality.

Why did highway robbery disappear?

A combination of factors led to the increase of highway robbers:

- The expansion of the system of **turnpikes**, manned and gated toll-roads, made it hard for a highwayman to escape unnoticed while making his getaway.
- Sir John Fielding's methods in the 1750s (see pages 30–1) had shown that it was possible to curb robbery on the king's highway through good policing.
- Some of the most dangerous open spaces near London, for example Finchley Common, were being occupied with new buildings.
- The stagecoach, a heavy and bulky carriage often without any form of springs, was introduced in Britain in 1640, which made roads busier than before.
- Severe punishments (execution was common) and The Highwayman Act of 1693, which, among other things, gave pardon to those highwaymen who betrayed their accomplices, also aided the decline of robberies on the highway.
- People began to make better use of banknotes, which were easier to trace than gold coins, and the first large British bank, The Bank of England, was set up in 1694.

BRAIN BOOST

Physical revision! Get hold of a bunch of sticky notes, give each room (or an area of a room) a specific 'Factor' (see the Introduction for the Big Factors page vii), then write down the various crimes on different sticky notes and attach these to furniture, walls etc. Now go around to each Factor room and read out all the notes aloud, removing them as you go along. When you have finished stick them back on and repeat the process regularly. You will be surprised how quickly you match power and government, poaching and smuggling with your bathroom!

2.18 Was the industrial city a breeding ground for crime?

LEARNING OBJECTIVES

In this lesson you will:

- understand why industrialisation led to more crime
- demonstrate how some factors link together.

ACTIVITIES

1   Compare Sources A and C. Has anything changed between the 1850s and 2006? Identify similarities and differences between the two sources.
2   Read Source B. What has the historian identified as contributing to the decrease in violent crimes?

SOURCE A

There were 757 deaths initially recorded as homicides in England and Wales based on cases recorded by the police in 2006–07, a decrease of two per cent since 2005–06.

- *75% of homicide victims were male.*
- *The most common method of killing, at 35%, involved a sharp instrument.*
- *There were 59 shooting victims in 2006–07 compared to 49 in 2005–06.*
- *Female victims were more likely to be killed by someone they knew: 68 per cent of female victims knew the main suspect compared to 44 per cent of male victims. Sixty-two per cent of victims aged under 16 knew the main suspect.*
- *Overall, the risk of being a victim of homicide was 13.7 per million population. Persons aged between 21 and 29 (inclusive) were the most at-risk age group, at 27 per million population.*

Home Office Statistical Bulletin 2006–07, Homicides Summary.

SOURCE B

The great majority of offenders brought before the courts during the nineteenth century, were prosecuted for either theft or physical assault of some sort. While the increase shown in the crime figures for the first part of the century may partly reflect an increasing desire to control the poor, the figures for the second half of the century suggest a general levelling out, even an overall decrease in theft and violence. This decrease coincides with increased court activity, with the spread and gradual professionalisation of the new police, and with an apparent increase in public cooperation with both courts and the police.

C. Bloom, *Violent London*, 2004.

SOURCE C

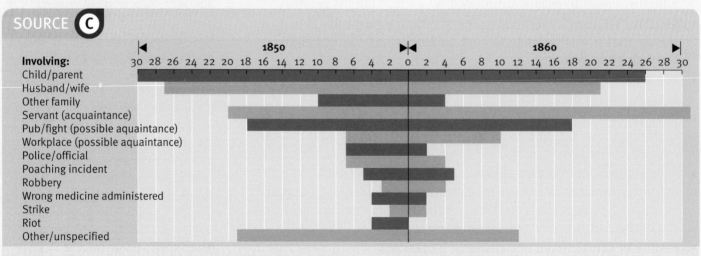

Graph of homicides and attempted homicides, 1850 and 1860.

ACTIVITIES

3 Study the information boxes which describe life in Industrial Britain.

a Choose which three boxes best support the idea that the industrial city was a breeding ground for crime

b Create an ideas map using each of the key factors, for example, crime, population and alcohol, and add a few notes about how you think these might have contributed to the increase in crime.

c Which parts of your ideas map link together? Draw a dotted arrow between the key factors that link, for example, population, poverty and alcohol, and then explain your reasons.

Life in the city

The problems were already becoming clear as early as 1808, when the poet Robert Southey wrote:

'The dwellings of the labouring manufacturers are in narrow streets and lanes, blocked up from light and air, crowded together because every inch of land is of such value that room for light and air cannot be afforded them. Here in Manchester, a great proportion of the poor lodge in cellars, damp and dark, where every kind of filth is suffered to accumulate because no exertions of domestic care can ever make such homes decent.'

New cities population growth

	1801	1851	1901
London	957	2362	4536
Birmingham	957	2362	4536
Manchester	71	233	523
Norwich	70	303	645
Bath	36	68	114
Brighton	33	54	50
Newcastle	7	70	123
Hull	30	85	240
Sunderland	25	67	240

The criminal class

Today we are concerned about 'organised crime'. In the 19th century, contemporaries debated the existence of professional criminals and the rather less precise 'criminal classes'. At the beginning of Victoria's reign in 1837 key individuals such as Edwin Chadwick, a social reformer, thought of criminal offenders as individuals in the lower end of the working class who loathed to do a decent day's work for a day's wage, and who preferred unemployment, drink and an easy life. Many people, especially the rich, were worried about the 'dangerous classes' who were thought to sneak around in the slums waiting for the opportunity for disorder and plunder and murder.

Poverty

W. Booth, *In Darkest England*, 1890

'I found the poor wretches by the score; almost every seat contained its full complement of six – some men, some women – all reclining in various postures and nearly all fast asleep... Here are scores of men lying side by side, huddled together for warmth, and of course, without any other covering than their ordinary clothing... Some have laid down a few pieces of waste paper, by way of taking the chill off the stones, but the majority are too tired, even for that, and the nightly toilet of most consists of first removing the hat, swathing the head in whatever old rag may be doing duty as a handkerchief, and then replacing the hat.'

Average age of death

	Manchester	Rutland
Professional person	38	52
Tradesmen and their families	20	41
Labourers and their families	17	38

Public hygiene and nutrition

Tuberculosis, 'the White Plague', was a remorseless killer of the urban poor, accounting for perhaps one-third of all deaths from disease in the Victorian period. Poor nutrition (probably less than two-thirds the calorific intake recommended by the Council of Nutrition today), in the context of hard physical labour, and some appalling industrial diseases ensured that the working class, particularly the poorer sections, were much worse off than their middle-class countrymen.

Alcohol

Alcohol was seen as the root of all evil in 19th-century Britain: from the increase in crime to the break-up of families. People thought that criminals committed crimes to feed their alcohol problem; that pubs were breeding grounds of thugs and that if someone lost their job they would 'hit the bottle'.

Crime

Despite the horrors of the Jack the Ripper murders of 1888, Victorian Britain was an ordered society. Crime, whether violent assault or theft, was uncommon despite the frenzied reporting of shocking events by the tabloid press. In reality, crime actually declined which contradicted the fear that greater **urbanisation** led to more criminality. Gun crime, to use one example, was a rare occurrence even in London in the 1800s.

Napoleonic War (1799–1815) and economic depression

When the war ended, approximately 200,000 soldiers returned home – many came to London. A large proportion of these turned to stealing to keep body and soul together. England experienced economic depression between 1815 and 1819, and the amount of recorded crimes increased significantly.

2.19 How did the government respond to 19th-century protests? The Peterloo Massacre

LEARNING OBJECTIVES

In this lesson you will:

- examine the events of the Peterloo Massacre and how the government responded
- select evidence to make a judgement about a past event.

ACTIVITIES

Read Source A.

1. What issues concern the Home Secretary?
2. What is his advice on how to respond to each of these issues?

On 8 August 1819 a letter was sent from the office of the Home Secretary, Lord Sidmouth, to the local authorities in Manchester in response to a planned meeting of large numbers of people who wanted parliamentary reform and an increase in the number of people who were allowed to vote.

SOURCE A

Sir,

Lord Sidmouth desires me to say that reflection convinces him the more strongly of the inexpediency [unsuitability] of attempting forcibly to prevent the meeting on Monday. Every discouragement and obstacle should be thrown in its way but his Lordship thinks that it would be imprudent to act up to the spirit of the advertisement [of mass arrests].

He has no doubt that you will make arrangements for obtaining evidence of what passes; that if any thing illegal is done or said it may be the subject of prosecution. But even if they should utter sedition [treasonous words], Lord Sidmouth is of opinion that it will be the wisest course to abstain from any endeavour [attempt] to disperse the mob, unless they should proceed to acts of felony or riot.

A letter sent to Manchester on behalf of Lord Sidmouth, the Home Secretary, 4 August 1819.

SOURCE B

Early in the afternoon, local magistrates called the cavalry to arrest two persons, Hunt and Johnson, who were on the stage; not a shot has been fired by the people against the troops. I have, however, great regret in stating that some of the unfortunate people who attended this meeting have suffered from sabre wounds, and many from the pressure of the crowd. One of the Manchester Yeomanry, if not dead, lies without hope of recovery. It is understood he was struck with a stone. One of the special constables has been killed.

Eyewitness account from Lieutenant-Colonel George L'Estrange, Commander of the Yeomanry at St Peter's Field.

The meeting was very well attended. Many people came to see the prominent speakers, including the famous speaker Henry Hunt, and it has been estimated that 60,000–80,000 people were at the meeting in St Peter's Field. The local magistrates, whose job it was to control such events, were so worried that the meeting might become a riot or even a rebellion that they called in 1500 regular and militia soldiers, and even two cannons. What was to follow became known as the 'Peterloo Massacre'.

After St Peter's Field had been cleared it became apparent that 11 people had died and between 400 and 600 wounded. The government was shocked and alarmed about the events in Manchester and was quick to respond.

The Yeomanry Cavalry made their charge with a most infuriate frenzy; they cut down men, women and children, indiscriminately, and appeared to have commenced a pre-meditated attack with the most insatiable thirst for blood and destruction.

As a proof of meditated murder on the part of the magistrates, every stone was gathered from the ground on the Friday and Saturday previous to the meeting, by scavengers sent there by the express command of the magistrates, that the populace might be rendered more defenceless.

Richard Carlile, an eyewitness and journalist, writing in *Sherwin's Weekly Political Register*, 18 August 1819. He reports the events in a quite different manner.

The reaction to Peterloo

The authorities responded by bringing several of those people involved to trial. Four of the Manchester Yeomanry were found not guilty of any wrongdoing and released. Nine of the protesters, including Henry Hunt, were charged with inciting treasonous acts (sedition). Five of these protesters were found guilty and each imprisoned for up to two-and-a-half years.

The government also wanted to crack down on reformers to prevent any possible uprising, and so passed a number of laws that became known as the Six Acts. These were aimed at stopping large meetings from happening, silencing radical newspapers and reducing the chance of armed rebellion.

The Six Acts

The *Newspaper and Stamp Duties Act* was aimed at the publishers of newspapers and pamphlets. They had to provide a deposit to guarantee their good behaviour. They were also required to pay more tax on their work.
The *Training Prevention Act* allowed for the arrest and transportation of anyone attending a meeting for the purpose of receiving training in weapons.
The *Seizure of Arms Act* allowed local magistrates to search private property for weapons, seize any they found and arrest the owners.
The *Seditious Meetings Prevention Act* meant that anyone who wanted to hold a meeting about either church or state matters where more than 50 people were going to attend had to gain the permission of a sheriff or magistrate. It also made it illegal for people to attend who did not live in the parish the meeting was in.
The *Blasphemous and Seditious Libels Act* amended the existing laws and allowed harsher sentences for the authors of writings deemed dangerous to the church or state. The maximum sentence was increased to 14 years' transportation.
The *Misdemeanors Act* reduced opportunities for bail and increased the speed of court procedures.

Work in groups of three and use the information in the lesson so far. You have been asked by Lord Sidmouth, the Home Secretary, to look into the events at St Peter's Field. He has asked three specific questions that you must answer.

3 What will be the focus of your enquiry?

4 Who do you think is to blame for the events?

5 What are your recommendations for following up Peterloo? These can include new laws, punishments, political reforms or anything similar.

Read through each of the Six Acts and decide whether or not each one could have prevented the Peterloo Massacre had they been in force beforehand. How fair do you think these laws were as a response to protests for parliamentary reform?

2.20 How did the government respond to 19th-century protests? The Rebecca Riots

LEARNING OBJECTIVES

In this lesson you will:

- examine the events of the Rebecca Riots and how the government responded
- compare and contrast past events to form a conclusion.

From 1839 to 1843 rural West Wales was the centre for a new wave of protest. The 'Rebecca Riots', as they were called, were a series of outbreaks of violence directed upon the toll gates of the area.

From the early 18th century the major roads in Britain had been administered by 'turnpike trusts'. The trustees in charge of these trusts had the right to set up toll gates, so anyone using that road had to pay a fee, which was supposed to go towards the maintenance of that road. However, by the 1830s it was felt by many that these toll gates were being used as a means to make money from local people rather than to maintain the roads.

The rural population of the area also had many other grievances that fed into the anger they directed towards the toll gates.

- The poor laws and union workhouses were seen as at best unhelpful to those struggling with falling livestock levels and poor harvests.
- About 80 per cent of the population in these areas were Nonconformist Christians who refused to follow the Anglican Church of England. They were angry that they still had to pay tithes and other taxes to fund a church they were not members of.

To disguise their identities while taking part in the attacks, the rioters would dress up in women's clothes. They referred to themselves as 'Rebecca and her daughters' – possibly a reference to a passage from the Bible.

SOURCE A

A mid-19th-century cartoon depicting the Rebecca Riots. The toll gate is marked with the various issues the rioters were opposed to. The gate they are attacking also represents the various issues that angered local people at the time.

SOURCE B

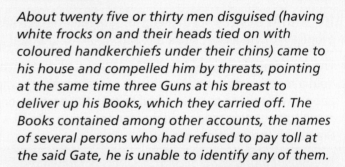

About twenty five or thirty men disguised (having white frocks on and their heads tied on with coloured handkerchiefs under their chins) came to his house and compelled him by threats, pointing at the same time three Guns at his breast to deliver up his Books, which they carried off. The Books contained among other accounts, the names of several persons who had refused to pay toll at the said Gate, he is unable to identify any of them.

Statement of William Rees, Toll Collector of Trevaughan Turnpike Gate, 15 August 1843.

How did the authorities respond?

The increasing number of attacks on the toll gates soon became a matter of real concern for the authorities., The Chief Constable of the Glamorgan police himself arrived to organise the enquiries in 1843. The initial questioning did not produce many details, but large rewards were offered for information.

This was soon to provide the names of many of the leaders of one of the attacks, who were promptly arrested and prosecuted. As the attacks on the toll houses became more violent, more criminal characters became involved in organising the attacks. This led to a loss of support from the local people, which in turn lead to more information being passed to the authorities, who were made aware of proposed meetings and planned attacks by the Rebeccaites.

Clashes between the rioters and the police and soldiers continued until 1843, when several ringleaders were arrested and tried. They were then transported to Australia, after which the protests began to subside. The government responded by appointing a Royal Commission to look into the toll roads and by 1844 new laws were passed and most of the toll gates were removed.

SOURCE

Enough has been done already to convince the Government of the great and universal discontent which your grievances have caused among you. They have sent down soldiers to keep the peace. I therefore entreat you not to meet together on Wednesday night. I have written for the soldiers to come here and prevent your doing any mischief if you should. Why, by your violence and absurdity, which can do no good, turn me from a friend to an enemy? Your conduct is childish and absurd, and not like men who have great objects to attain. Why will you exhibit folly when wisdom is required? The penalty for pulling down a Turnpike House is TRANSPORTATION FOR LIFE.

Extract from a letter from the high sheriff of Cardiganshire to the Rebeccaites, 1843.

ACTIVITIES

1 Working with a partner, come up with a list of five actions that you would take to solve the problem of the Rebeccaites and the attacks on the toll gates.

2 Make a list of each step that the authorities took in response to the events of the Rebecca Riots.

3 How effective do you think each step was?

4 Was this the most sensible course of action that could have been taken?

5 Look back at how the authorities reacted to the Peterloo Massacre. Make a list of the differences in reaction by the authorities between the Peterloo Massacre and the Rebecca Riots?

6 What do you think made the biggest difference to the different outcomes of the Peterloo Massacre and the Rebecca Riots? Remember to back up your argument with details from the sources and your own knowledge.

2.21 Has crime increased rapidly since 1900?

LEARNING OBJECTIVES

In this lesson you will:

- learn about the changing nature of crime in the 20th century
- synthesise information to create a conclusion about crime rates in the 20th century.

SOURCE A

In most cases, all the figures show is that the police are noting down more crimes in their notebooks than they used to, not that the number of crimes has increased. The irony is that the more efficient the police become, the higher the recorded crime figures rise.

J.M. Coutts, *Social Issues*, 1985.

Crime figures

Violent crime has amounted to 5–6 per cent of all crime from 1901–2000.

The number of burglaries went up by 18 per cent in the 20th century, but the number of reports increased by 100 per cent.

A The police record more crime then ever before.

B It is estimated that up to 60 per cent of crime is unreported. This is known as the 'dark figure'.

C Most crime is committed by young men under the age of 21.

D The police have become more trusted and efficient.

E In the 19th century there were 15 murders per 1 million people.

F In the 1980s there were 11 murders per 1 million people.

Where does this leave our opinions of crime and its changing nature in the 20th century? It is certain that the press and media want to believe that violence and crime are everywhere – in 2008 the main focus has been knife crime, particularly in London.

Why has this happened?

There are several factors that can help to explain these changes.

The first is events that occurred in the 20th century and the impact they had on crime.

The events might help to explain why crime was falling in the first four decades of the 20th century. However, new technology was creating new crimes. As people began to own motor vehicles, others began to steal them. Also, new crimes such as speeding and dangerous driving were created and this had an impact on the statistics.

Some other factors are not as clear as they might appear. For example, the depression in the 1930s did not necessarily mean that people turned to crime. In fact, it was the older and skilled workers who suffered most and they are the least likely category of men to commit crime. Also, the prosperity of the 1950s actually led to a sharp increase in crime. As people began to buy and own more expensive goods, there was more to steal and so the decade saw a 20 per cent increase in crimes against property.

ACTIVITIES

1 Draw around your hands and label the left one 'Crime is higher and more violent' and label the right one 'Crime is not higher and more violent'.

2 Add information from these pages to your diagram, putting one piece of evidence in each finger.

Type of crime	1993 Police Statistic	1993 BCS Statistic	% reported to police
Burglary	727,000	1,754,000	69
Wounding	169,000	692,000	54
Robbery and theft from a person	102,000	835,000	32

Some results from the British Crime Survey (BCS), 1994.

One of the most remarkable features of the Depression has been the absence of serious crime among unemployed workers.

George Orwell, *The Road to Wigan Pier*, 1937.

A political row erupted last night as new crime figures for England and Wales showed the largest drop since 1954. Reported crime fell by 5.5 per cent overall, but violent and sexual offences rose sharply, according to Home Office figures.

Police recorded 5,365,400 crimes in the year to June 1994 – 311,500 fewer than the year before. The Government heralded the figures as 'encouraging'.

From *The Times*, September 1994.

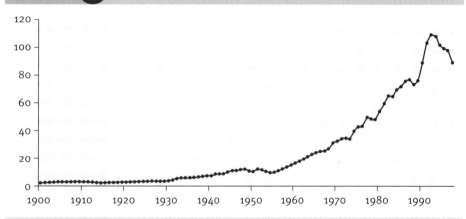

Offences known to the police (per thousand of population) in England and Wales 1900–1997.

The British Crime Survey estimates unreported crime; in 1997 56% of crimes were not reported to the police. In earlier years, this figure was probably higher and accounts for some of the increase.

A Century of Change: Trends in UK statistics since 1900, *A House of Commons research paper.*

ACTIVITIES

3 When would you expect crime to be higher and when would you expect it to be lower?

4 Rank order the following reasons for the changing nature of crime. Say why you have placed them in the order you have.
   a There is more crime because more is reported.
   b There is more crime because the police record more.
   c There is more crime because more people are committing it.
   d There is more crime in times of poverty.
   e There is more crime because we have more young people around.
   f There is more crime because there are more vulnerable people around.

2.22 Anarchy, annoying or moral crusade? The Suffragettes

LEARNING OBJECTIVES

In this lesson you will:
- find out about the Suffragettes' struggle for the vote and the protests of the workers in 1926
- deconstruct interpretations of protesters and suggest why they have been created.

KEY WORDS

Suffrage – *the right to vote in elections.*

Suffragists/suffragettes – *name given to women who campaigned for the vote.*

WSPU – *group set up by leading campaigner Emmeline Pankhurst to actively campaign for votes for women.*

The suffragettes and the struggle for the vote

At the turn of the 20th century, the role of women in society was still a relatively closed one. Women were expected to raise a family and be a good wife – nothing more. Some years before, women had fought for and gained the right to have places in universities and roles as professionals, such as teachers and doctors. This, however, was not matched by a greater role in the way the country was run. Neither did it improve their position in society. Women were still seen as the property of men and expected to be proper and well behaved at all times. For the majority of young women, the best that could be hoped for was to gain a position in service at a big house. The worst would be to get pregnant before marriage; girls in this situation would expect for their babies to be raised by another family member or taken away. Up to the 1930s, there were cases of young girls being sent to asylums for having sex before marriage.

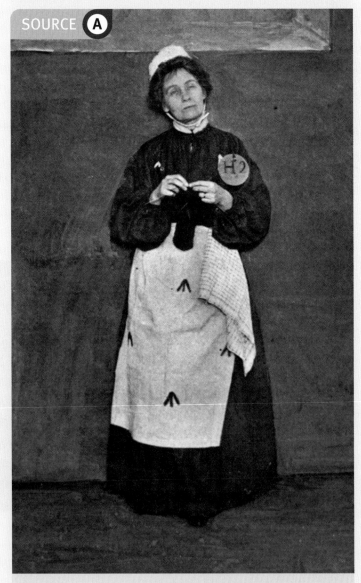

SOURCE **A**

A suffragette in prison uniform, 1909.

Stage one: Persuasion and reason

However, the desires women had for careers and equal rights had grown throughout the late 1800s. By 1897 there was a united movement that campaigned for women to get the vote, under the banner of the National Union of Women's **Suffrage** Societies (NUWSS). The society had over 500 branches across the country and believed in democratic principles. They tried to persuade and influence politicians by holding meetings and marches and writing books, pamphlets and a newspaper.

The story of Christobel Pankhurst's first trip to prison

It seemed likely that the Liberal Party would win the 1906 election and the leading **suffragettes** wanted to know if the new government was in favour of votes for women. Christobel Pankhurst, daughter of the WSPU leader Emmeline, found out that a leading politician, Sir Edward Grey, was speaking at the Manchester Free Trade Hall and made up her mind to confront him. With her friend, Annie Kerry, she made a large banner that read, 'Will you give votes for women?' However, Christobel had bigger plans: she told Annie, 'I shall sleep in prison tonight.'

The two suffragettes, as the *Daily Mail* had started to call them, sat in the Liberal Meeting and waited for questions to start. Christobel stood up and asked her question about votes for women. There was a mixed reaction, with some saying 'let the lady speak' and others urging her to be quiet. At first, Grey refused to answer the question, but later he said that votes for women was not a party political matter and so he refused to comment.

On hearing this, Christobel and Annie unfurled their banner and waved it vigorously, while shouting their slogan. Several men came over and evicted them, but Christobel wanted a bigger reaction. She pretended to spit at a policeman who was outside and so she was arrested. She was taken to Strangeways prison and locked up in a small cell. She was the first of hundreds of suffragettes to be arrested and sent to prison.

Stage two: 'Deeds not words'

This style proved too slow for some and so Emmeline Pankhurst established the Women's Social and Political Union (**WSPU**) in 1903. Its slogan was 'Deeds not Words'. The WSPU took a more militant line and fought for their rights with acts of arson, by chaining themselves to railings and hunger strikes. Their activities reached a peak in 1910.

SOURCE

When the Suffragettes began their campaign they were mistaken for notoriety hunters, featherheads, flibbertigibbets. Their proceedings were not taken seriously. Now they have proved they are in dead earnest, they have frightened the Government, they have broken the law, they have made votes for women practical politics.

From an editorial in the *Daily Mail*, 1906.

SOURCE

We're clearly soldiers in petticoats
And dauntless crusaders for woman's votes
Though we adore men individually
We agree that as a group they're rather stupid!

Cast off the shackles of yesterday!
Shoulder to shoulder into the fray!
Our daughters' daughters will adore us
And they'll sign in grateful chorus
'Well done, Sister Suffragette!'

From Kensington to Billingsgate
One hears the restless cries!
From ev'ry corner of the land:
'Womankind, arise!'
Political equality and equal rights with men!
Take heart! For Missus Pankhurst has been clapped in irons again!

No more the meek and mild subservients we!
We're fighting for our rights, militantly!
Never you fear!

So, cast off the shackles of yesterday!
Shoulder to shoulder into the fray!
Our daughters' daughters will adore us
And they'll sign in grateful chorus
'Well done! Well done!
Well done Sister Suffragette!'

Lyrics from 'Sister Suffragette', a song from the film *Mary Poppins* (1964).

Shout, shout, up with your song!
Cry with the wind, for the dawn is breaking.
March, march, swing you along,
Wide blows our banner and hope is waking.
Song with its story, dreams with their glory,
Lo! They call and glad is their word.
Forward! Hark how it swells,
Thunder of freedom, the voice of the Lord!

Long, long, we in the past.
Cower'd in dread from the light of Heaven,
Strong, strong stand we at last,
Fearless in faith and with sight new given.
Strength with its beauty, life with its duty,
(Hear the voice oh, hear and obey).
These, these beckon us on,
Open your eyes to the blaze of day!

Comrades, ye who have dared.
First in the battle to strive and sorrow.
Scorned, spurned, naught have ye cared,
Raising your eyes to a wider morrow.
Ways that are weary, days that are dreary,
Toil and pain by faith ye have borne.
Hail, hail, victors ye stand,
Wearing the wreath that the brave have worn!
March, march, many as one,
Shoulder to shoulder and friend to friend.

Lyrics from a 1911 song *The March of the Women*, by Ethel Smyth (leader of the Holloway Prison Suffragette Choir).

Suffragette poster about force feeding, 1910.

ACTIVITIES

1   What are the main differences between the lyrics in the two songs (Sources C and D) and where are they similar? Create a Venn diagram to compare and contrast the two.

2   Look at where these two sources come from. How does this information affect how you view these sources?

3   What were the suffragettes hoping to achieve by publishing the poster in Source E?

Stage three: Cat and Mouse

On 1 July 1909, the suffragette Marion Wallace Dunlop refused to eat prison food. It was the same every day after this, no matter what the guards and doctors put in front of her. Once they asked her what she wanted to eat and she replied, 'My determination!' After 91 hours without food she collapsed and the authorities let her go.

Other suffragettes started to use the same method of protest, so the government decided to force feed them. This involved liquids being poured down a tube which was put in their mouth and down their throat. It took up to seven wardens to hold down a prisoner being force fed.

After several suffragettes almost died in prison, the government decided that they should be released if they went on hunger strike. When they were well again, they could be re-arrested and taken back to prison. Of course, as soon as they got back to Holloway prison, they went back on hunger strike and the whole process started again. The new law about releasing hunger strikers and re-arresting them was called the Cat and Mouse Act, 1913.

Stage four: Violence against others

By 1913 the suffragettes were ready to step up the campaign again. They were now engaged with activities like cutting telegraph wires, setting fire to post boxes, vandalising sports grounds and interrupting major events. They even went as far as trying to injure politicians with axes and bombs. The most famous incident is that of Emily Davison who died while trying to stop the king's horse in the 1913 Derby race.

The Prime Minister, Herbert Asquith, now faced a serious dilemma: most Liberal MPs were in favour of votes for women and there was a good chance that a new bill might pass Parliament. However, he did not want to be seen to be giving in to violent protest, especially since there was trouble in Ireland with people who had taken up arms to try to get the British to leave. Asquith continued with the Cat and Mouse Act and made sure that all those suffragettes committing serious acts were locked up in prison.

It was at this point that the First World War began and both organisations for women's votes told their followers to end their actions against the government and do their bit for the war.

ACTIVITY

4   The title of this lesson is 'Anarchy, annoying or moral crusade?' How should the protests of the suffragettes be viewed? Create a chart similar to the one below and make a case for all three viewpoints about the suffragettes.

Anarchy (no rules or order from the authorities)	Annoying (stopped society from running in a normal way)	Moral crusade (had a serious principle to uphold and did it without fear)
	Cartoon in Source F says children were not washed.	

GradeStudio

How useful is Source F in explaining attitudes towards the suffragettes? Use the source and your own knowledge to explain your answer.

Examiner's tip

In questions that ask you to assess the usefulness of a source, you will need to do TWO things – show understanding of the source and knowledge of events and opinions connected to the topic, AND to use that knowledge and understanding to *EXPLAIN WHY* the source is and is not useful.

It is important to do more than just describe what the source shows – describing is NOT the same as explaining.

*   Use phrases like, 'This information suggests that...'
*   For such questions, make sure your answer includes words such as 'useful' and 'not useful'.
*   The best answers will have points to support both 'useful' and 'not useful' sides of the argument.

Now try answering the question by breaking it down into four parts as follows.

a   What does Source F show?
b   What does Source F tell us about the attitude of some men and the police towards suffragettes?
c   What else do you know about this topic that supports or contradicts the information in Source F?
d   Conclude your answer about how useful the source is.

There was clearly a difference of opinion about whether women should get the vote. Bills supporting the suffragists were introduced to Parliament in 1907, 1908 and twice in 1910, but all of them were defeated.

Without the support of most MPs it was impossible to get a bill for women's suffrage through Parliament. Therefore, the suffragettes stepped up their campaign and took it further.

SOURCE F

A SUFFRAGIST GOING TO PRISON.

Magazine cartoon from 1909.

2.23 Anarchy, annoying or moral crusade? The General Strike

Victory in the First World War (1914–18) had not brought about any significant changes to society. The level of sacrifice in the trenches had hit Britain hard and so people expected that those returning from military duty would step back on British soil and be given 'a fit land for heroes to live in'. This did not emerge and there are two main reasons for this.

1 **Competition from abroad**

The traditional industries like coal, steel and textiles faced cheaper products from abroad. The rise of America and Japan and the quick recovery of Germany meant that there were fewer opportunities to sell goods than people had anticipated.

2 **The collapse of world trade**

The war had disrupted trade and it was slow to recover. Countries were not able to produce as much as they had before 1914 and so they could not afford to buy as much from Britain. For example, orders of Canadian grain were down and so Canada had less to spend on manufactured goods from Britain.

The decline in trade meant that industries were under strain. Workers were being sacked and wages reduced because bosses could not afford to keep payments at the same levels. There was a series of strikes for better pay and job security, such as the miners strike of 1921 and the rail strike of 1924, but the most serious was the General Strike of 1926. In all these events there was a growing sense of solidarity between working men in different industries. For example, in 1921, the 'Triple Alliance' was formed, with the miners, the railwaymen and the dockers agreeing to support each other. This did not work in 1921, because when the miners started their strike, the other two unions backed down. However, by 1926 they were ready to stand united.

The General Strike occurred in May 1926 and lasted for nine days. Most of Britain's workers were out on strike and it was well supported.

SOURCE A

I was a miner
I was a docker
I was a railway man
Between the wars;
I raised a family
In times of austerity
With sweat at the foundry
Between the wars.

I paid the union and as times got harder
I looked to the government to help the working man
And they brought prosperity down at the armoury
We're arming for peace, me boys
Between the wars.

I kept the faith and I kept voting
Not for the iron fist but for the helping hand
For theirs is a land with a wall around it
And mine is a faith in my fellow man
Theirs is a land of hope and glory
Mine is the green field and the factory floor
Theirs are the skies all dark with bombers
And mine is the peace we knew
Between the wars.

Call up the craftsmen
Bring me the draftsmen
Build me a path from cradle to grave
And I'll give my consent
To any government
That does not deny a man a living wage.

Go find the young men never to fight again
Bring up the banners from the days gone by
Sweet moderation
Heart of this nation
Desert us not, we are
Between the wars.

Modern song lyrics from *Between the Wars*, written by Billy Bragg.

What reason could there be for food being escorted by armoured cars?

ACTIVITIES

1. What messages about the working class is Billy Bragg trying to give?
2. Which viewpoint in the question would the writer of the song most support: *anarchy, annoying or moral crusade*?
3. Sort the 16 statements below into three categories: anarchy, annoying and moral crusade.
4. Overall, which interpretation of the three do you favour the most? Why?
5. What caused the government to take a hard line with the protests of the suffragettes and the striking workers?

The army stepped in and made sure that food supplies reached the shops. This meant that life could continue in a fairly normal way.

Volunteers, mostly middle class and university students, were brought in to run public transport.

The miners were facing poor conditions and worsening pay.

Before the General Strike, the government had been topping up the wages of the miners.

The Trades Union Congress (TUC) called for a strike to happen and said that it should involve all workers.

Special constables were created to assist other officers. Some only took the job so that they could smash the strike. They were found to be members of the British Fascist Party.

Punch ran a cartoon called 'The lever breaks' which accused the strikers of trying to smash constitutional government.

Print workers at the *Daily Mail* refused to print an editorial that read, 'The general strike is not an industrial dispute; it is a revolutionary movement, intended to inflict suffering on the great mass of innocent persons in the community…'

The army and navy were called in to help ensure that order was kept and food got to the people.

The organisers of the General Strike did not let refuse collectors join in.

The TUC argued that if the working man let the miners have low pay and poor conditions, other industries would quickly follow.

The British Worker newspaper reported, 'A procession of transport workers… marched in fours to Brockwell Park. The immense crowd in the park gave a clear indication of where the sympathies of the British nation lie.'

The TUC aimed to cause problems for other industries and hoped the bosses would force mine owners to back down.

There were at least 2.5 million workers on strike.

The British Gazette newspaper accused the strikers of trying to set up a communist committee, just like in Russia.

Winston Churchill suggested that tanks and snipers be used to stop the General Strike and assassinate its leadership.

2.24 Are young people ruining society?

LEARNING OBJECTIVES

In this lesson you will:
- develop a critical understanding of an issue
- question the opinions of experts.

GETTING STARTED

13 July 2008

REVEALED:
THE TRUTH ABOUT KNIFE CRIME

IT HAS SOARED BY 35 PER CENT IN SOME PARTS OF BRITAIN

By Tom Harper

The full scale of Britain's growing knife crime menace is today exposed by The Mail on Sunday. Our new figures show that almost every major city is facing soaring levels of stabbings and knifepoint muggings – casting doubt on Home Secretary Jacqui Smith's reassurances about the safety of our streets.

The data shows the problem is not confined to London – where 53 people have been stabbed to death so far this year – but is a rising concern in most urban areas.

Taken from the website of the Daily Mail, 13 July 2008.

How do reports like this one affect:

a you

b younger brothers and sisters

c your parents and adult neighbours

d your grandparents?

Look at the statistics in Source A.

SOURCE A

Year	Number of recorded violent attacks
1945	5000
1960	16,000
1991	200,000

Changes in the number of violent attacks recorded, 1945–91.

It is clear that more violent attacks are happening, but who is committing them? You will probably not be surprised to learn that 65 per cent of all crime is committed by men under the age of 25 and 50 per cent of crime by men under 20 years. The most common age for a criminal is 15–16 years. Men commit six times as much crime as women, but the number of girls (aged 14–15) being convicted is also rising.

Types of crime committed by young people

There are a number of crimes where most of the offences are committed by young people. These include:

- joyriding
- shoplifting
- vandalism
- gang fighting
- football hooliganism
- drug and alcohol abuse
- anti-social behaviour.

Case study 1: Vandalism

It would seem that graffiti and vandalism happen on a daily basis in every town. The statistics show a sharp rise in vandalism since 1977. Does this mean that after this date young people suddenly started to smash up things?

Actually, no. Vandalism is nothing new – the Romans had to deal with exactly the same problems (see page 42). Before 1977, the police only recorded vandalism that caused more than £20 of damage. After that date, they had to record everything. This led to an immediate increase of 15,000 cases in that year alone. More vandalism may be committed, but it is also true that much more is recorded too.

Case study 2: Football hooliganism

Just like vandalism, violence at sporting events is nothing new. The Ancient world was full of incidents and there are documented cases of fighting at football matches before the First World War. However, there was a huge increase in the later part of the 20th century. This came to a head in 1985 when 38 people died and 400 were injured at the Heysel stadium in Belgium during a European Championship game involving Liverpool. This resulted in a ban of English clubs from all European competitions. Since then clubs have taken measures to stamp out problems involving fighting and racism in their grounds, and the issue no longer dominates the sport like it did in the 1980s and 1990s.

Why?

There has been a range of studies to help identify why young people turn to crime. This has led to disagreement among experts. Some believe it is a product of society and shows that traditional values about family and community are in decline. Others blame poverty, saying that in some areas young people see no way of making a decent living and so turn to crime. Others point to the fact that the police and prison do not do enough to discourage young people, and that they know little will be done if they commit crime. Another group blames the media and says that TV and film glamorise crime, along with music and popular culture.

ACTIVITIES

1 In a group of four, create a definition for each of the crimes in the list 'Types of Crime Committed by Young People'. Try to explain why young people become involved in these activities. What do you think of police and government efforts to stamp them out?

2 Create a survey that could be given to young people to find out why they commit crime. Make two questions to fit under each of the following headings:

   a parents and their attitudes

   b drug abuse

   c respect for local community

   d fear of getting caught and punished

   e wealth and poverty

   f education and future prospects

   g the media.

   You could carry out the survey and ask people which factors they feel are most important in causing juvenile (young persons') crime. Choose the three factors that you feel are most responsible and create an argument to convince the experts that you are right.

VOICE YOUR OPINION!

Here is a quotation about newspapers from a media studies book published in 1989: 'The broadsheets report about three times the actual proportion of violent crime and the tabloids about ten times.' The picture of the world that one gets from crime news is that it is a very violent place. Inflated perceptions of the level of violence create pressures for something to be done.

How far do you think this view is true of young people? Do we read a distorted amount about them and therefore have the wrong impression of their actions in society? Give the quotation an accuracy rating, 1–5 stars, and explain why you have awarded this mark.

2.25 Get your sources sorted!

Why was there a 'Battle of Trafalgar' in 1990?

LEARNING OBJECTIVES

In this lesson you will:

- understand the reasons for the Poll Tax Riots
- identify and explain consequences of the riots.

The 'Poll Tax', officially called 'Community Charge', was introduced by Margaret Thatcher's Conservative government in 1988. This new tax replaced the local rates tax with a per head (poll) charge that each adult had to pay. It was seen as regressive, that is, taxing the poor more than the rich.

The poll tax enraged people because it was a levy on individuals regardless of means. Disorder began in central London following a demonstration in Trafalgar Square. The number of protesters was far larger than anticipated – nearly 100,000 people. The demonstration had started peacefully but things spiralled out of control. Some commentators claim the police used unnecessary force and some demonstrators turned violent.

SOURCE A

A protester is arrested as fire crews try to get the burning buildings under control during the Poll Tax Riots.

SOURCE B

Gangs of rioters and looters were rampaging across London's West End last night after Britain's biggest anti-Poll Tax rally erupted into violence. Police lost control after what had been a peaceful protest degenerated into an evening of chaos. At least 132 people were hurt and 341 arrested. Fifty-seven police and 75 demonstrators were taken to hospital and 20 police horses were hurt.

By 7pm, roads leading from the rally in Trafalgar Square featured fires, overturned police vans, burnt-out cars and widespread looting.

Article from the *Times*, 1 April 1990.

SOURCE C

The Poll Tax was a flat rate tax. It was not based on ability to pay. Everyone over eighteen was liable. Rich and poor the same. The millionaire paid the same as a toilet attendant... The Prime Minister Margaret Thatcher and her millionaire husband paid the same as their gardener. The tax was officially dubbed the Poll Tax because of its similarity to a tax introduced in 1381 which eventually led to the Peasant's Revolt.

Poll Tax Rebellion, Danny Burns, Secretary of the Avon Foundation of the Anti-Poll Tax Unions.

Why was the Poll Tax withdrawn?

The campaign against the Poll Tax gathered pace, and by the summer of 1990 more than 14 million people were refusing to pay it. The riots probably did not lead to the abandonment of the tax, but provoked questions about the nature of protest and how democratically elected governments should react. It was mass civil disobedience that eventually brought about the end of the Poll Tax – from local MPs to grassroots organisations in local communities who all refused to pay. In November 1990, Margaret Thatcher, who refused to withdraw the tax, resigned. It was abandoned in 1992 and replaced with the council tax.

ACTIVITIES

You are working as a journalist for an online magazine and have been asked to interview Danny Burns, an anti-Poll Tax protester at the time of the protests. You will only have five minutes talking to him, so it is important to have a list of questions ready prior to the interview.

1 Create a table like the one below and write down five questions that you would like to ask to find out about the protest.

Who?	What?	When?	Why?	Where?

2 Now try to find the answers to your questions in the sources. How different do you think his answers would have been if he had been working for the Prime Minister, Margaret Thatcher?

Answering a utility question

This exercise will help you to plan out and write a top-level answer for a utility question.

Study Source D. How useful is this source as evidence about the attitudes towards poll tax protesters? Use the source and your knowledge to explain your answer. **[5 marks]**

Step 1

Read the question and underline what it is asking you to do. What do you know already? Annotate your thoughts about people's general attitudes towards poll tax protest. What do you think?

Step 2

Find some positive points that show the source is useful. You could look at the content of the source or what type of source it is (the attribute).

For example: 'The source is useful because it shows us that Ramsell was not really considered to be a hardened criminal.'

Find two more points that prove it is a useful source.

Step 3

Find some (negative) points that show the source is not useful. Again, you could look at the content of the source or the attribute.

For example: 'However, this source was published by the *Socialist Worker* newspaper, which was very critical of the community charge in general so Ramsell might be bending the truth to make himself look good.'

Find two more points.

Step 4

Look at the viewpoint the source tries to portray and evaluate this. Every source has a viewpoint and if you can recognise this and still see positive and negative points then you will get top marks.

For example: 'The author conveys the message that many people regarded poll tax protesters in a good light as Ramsell received many letters of support whilst in prison. Although the poll tax demonstrations became a wider grass-roots movement of civil disobedience, many people would not have been supportive of Ramsell's cause...'

Other prisoners were quite supportive – though they found it strange that someone had been sent down for a political campaign.

I got tons of mail and support. The coppers who were guarding the cells were amazed at the amount of mail they had to deliver.

I never paid the poll tax. It was not a pleasant experience, but I don't have any regrets.

Phil Ramsell, Poll Tax prisoner. He was sentenced to 28 days' imprisonment for not paying his Poll Tax; The *Socialist Worker* (issue 1946), 9 April 2005.

Grade Studio

Examiner's tips

- The key to 'How useful' questions is to show both positive and negative points. All sources are useful; even if the writer may appear to be biased, the source will still give you a viewpoint of a particular person or group. You need to find at least two positive and two negative points in order to create a balanced answer.
- Get into a habit of considering:
  - who has written the source
  - what type of source is it
  - what is the purpose of the source.

  If you do this then your analysis will be more rigorous and it will be easier to critically evaluate the source, which means higher marks!

2.26 What was the impact of the death of Jean Charles de Menezes?

LEARNING OBJECTIVES

In this lesson you will:

- analyse the different degrees of impact of the Menezes shooting
- explain how laws and policing have developed since the bombings on 7 July 2005.

GETTING STARTED

How do you think the London bombings of July 2007 led to the Menezes shooting?

Electrician Jean Charles de Menezes was shot dead on 22 July 2005, by police who mistook him for one of four would-be suicide bombers who had attacked London's transport system the previous day. Immediately after the shooting, Scotland Yard said the shooting had been directly linked to their anti-terrorist operation and that Menezes had refused to obey police instructions. It later emerged that Menezes was not the suspect they thought he was. His death had been a mistake. The police accepted full responsibility for their actions. What was the impact of this tragic story?

SOURCE A

One of the damaged tube trains immediately after the 7 July bombings.

SOURCE B

'I shouted "armed police" [and] at the same time brought my gun up from my leg and pointed it at his head area'.

'He continued to move towards me... it was at that stage I thought: "He is going to detonate, he is going to kill us and I have to act now in order to stop this from happening"... If I didn't act members of the public would be killed, my colleagues would be killed and I would be killed. I had a duty to protect the public.'

A firearms officer involved in the shooting. The *Guardian*, Saturday 25 October 2008.

London bombings

During morning rush hour of the 7 July 2005, London witnessed a series of explosions on its public transport system, which left more than 50 people dead and 700 injured. A fortnight later on 21 July, public transport was attacked yet again, this time by four coordinated explosions. Unlike the 7 July, these attacks did not cause the mass murder that had been intended because only the detonators exploded which led to just one person suffering minor injuries.

ACTIVITIES

What impact did the July bombings have on Britain?

1 Read each information box on the following page and decide if it caused:

   a short-term impact (effect on the day)

   b medium-term impact (effect over the following weeks/months)

   c long-term impact (wider effect over years).

2 Summarise these key points in a table.

3 *'The shooting of Jean Charles de Menezes has had no effect on policing in the UK.'*

   Using what you have studied in this lesson explain whether you agree with this statement. Give reasons for your answer.

The Terrorism Act was made law on 30 March 2006 and covered:
- **Encouragement to Terrorism.** For example, incitement or encouragement to others to commit acts of terrorism.
- **Spreading Terrorist Publications.** For example, selling publications that encourage terrorism, or help terrorists.
- **Terrorist training offences**.

The Menezes family were offered almost £585,000 compensation by the police. The family's campaign, Justice4Jean, to prosecute officers involved in the shooting continued for several years.

'London bombs take toll on tourism. The number of visitors from abroad to London fell sharply in the wake of last July's bombings, official figures show.' **BBC News Online, January 2006**

The Home Office introduced a new counter-terrorism policy or PPPP:
- Prevent
- Pursue
- Protect
- Prepare.

The Health Protection Agency found that 80 per cent of people involved in the attacks had suffered 'severe psychological distress'.

Hundreds of schools in London were closed on the Friday (8 July) following the bomb attacks on public transport.

After the 9/11 terrorist attacks stock markets around the world fell sharply and stayed down, and the war against terrorism dominated the public mood. After 7 July, an initial fall in share prices was largely reversed later the same day, and had recovered completely by the end of the following day (7–8 July).

Prices at a number of London's hotels increased by more than double on the 7 July as people were stranded in London.

The original draft of the Terrorism Act 2006 stated that suspects could be held for 90 days before being charged. This was amended to 28 days after pressure from backbench MPs.

The Home Secretary said on balance he believed ID cards would help rather than hinder the ability to deal with particular terrorist threats (8 July).

A detailed report into the 7 July 2005 bomb attacks was published on 11 May 2006 by the Parliamentary Intelligence and Security Committee.

Before the 2006 Terrorism Act, terror suspects could only be held for 14 days before being charged. The Act extended this to 28 days.

The Parliamentary Intelligence and Security Committee reported (July 2006): 'Efforts to improve cooperation with intelligence services abroad must also be at the heart of future efforts to beat international terrorism.'

Asked if the bombings would lead to civil liberties being curtailed, the Home Secretary, Mr Charles Clarke, stated: 'I always hope not.' Mr Clarke also said that the use of identity cards would not have stopped the London bombings (8 July).

Everyone over the age of 16 applying for a passport will have their details – including fingerprints and facial scans – added to a National Identity register from 2011–12. The first identity cards will be issued to non-EU foreign nationals coming to work in the UK in 2008. **BBC News 6 March 2008**

From 2009, about 200,000 airport workers in the UK will have to get identity cards as a condition of employment.

Charlie 12, the name given to a police officer involved in the Menezes shooting to protect his identity, had been a specialist firearms officer since 1998 and had never fired a gun at a suspect before. On 22 July 2005 he was informed that his team would be involved in an anti-terrorist operation and that there was a real danger that there could be extreme loss of life. Later, over the radio he heard: 'All units state red, state red.' A few minutes later Menezes was dead. At midday the next day Charlie 12 discovered he had killed the wrong man.

The Brazilian government released a statement expressing its shock at the killing of Menezes, saying that it looked forward 'to receiving the necessary explanation from the British authorities on the circumstances which led to this tragedy' (23 July 2005).

On 29 September 2008, artist Mark McGowan 're-enacted' the Menezes shooting in protest because: '… people are distracted by things like the X Factor and Christmas, so I'm doing this as a reaction' (Friday, 28 November 2008).

Putting it all together

You have now completed this chapter, which has focused on the changing nature of protest. You have also had practice in answering questions designed to prepare you for your exam. Below is an example of one type of exam question, with some hints to help you write a top-scoring answer.

a Explain why political crimes have made such an impact on Government since 1900. **[7 marks]**

Examiner's tip

Before you answer the question, look carefully at some of the issues that could be worth thinking about in the chart below. Then read the candidate's answer. Using the chart and the simplified mark scheme opposite it, can you spot why the candidate moved up the levels?

What should I write about?	Exemplar answer	Structure and tips
Introduction Begin by discussing what forms the three protests took and compare them.	For example '*All three methods of protest, however tragic, have changed the way the government reacts to dissent and also raise issues about what the public is willing to accept from a democratically elected government.*'	Explain your definition of the question. This will make it easier to write and get you thinking about the issue(s) from the start.
PARAGRAPH 1 Explain the cause and reaction to each protest briefly and identify one or two main factors that contributed to this.	For example '*The Poll Tax Riot enraged people as it was a tax on individuals regardless of means and became a mass grass-roots movement involving millions of people. By contrast, the conscientious objectors of the First and Second World Wars, received little sympathy from the rest of the population as…*'	Write about each of the protests and explain the main differences and consider what caused them and what reactions they had.
		At the end of your paragraph, create a mini-conclusion by referring back to the question.
PARAGRAPH 2 *Impact* Analyse each protest's impact on both law-making and law-enforcement.	For example '*The 7 July attacks generated widespread panic in the country and the government took action almost instantly over the way we travel as well as providing the police with new powers. For example…*'	Write about each of the points and think about the **different degrees of impact**: long/medium-term and short-term impact.
		At the end of your paragraph, create a mini-conclusion by referring back to the question.
CONCLUSION • What do you think? • How has each one changed the way democratically elected governments react to dissent? • What evidence do you have to back up the conclusion you reach?	For example '*Clashes between anti-poll tax demonstrators and police highlighted issues about police methods which were developed and introduced during the 1980s to deal with mass protests… The long-term impact of the 7 July bombings have been the Terrorist Act of 2006 and discussion about biometric ID cards which will…*'	Try to make a reasoned judgement on the question. Support it with evidence from your own knowledge, and, if possible, give a few good quotations from the sources.

Fact file

In the exam, you will be asked to answer two questions from Section A, the Development Study: a source-based question and a structured question. The structured question is divided into three parts – **a**, **b** and **c**. In this Grade Studio we will be looking at how to produce a top-level answer for the **c** type of question. The **c** question has 8 marks.

Simplified mark scheme

Level 1   Makes general assertions OR describes.   **[1 mark]**
Valid but general answers – no specific contextual knowledge.
For example, '*All the protests changed the way the government reacts to dissent, for example the Poll Tax Riots...,*

Level 2   Identifies and describes impact.   **[2–3 marks]**
Specific contextual knowledge demonstrated but no explanation.
For example, '*The government changed their policies towards COs drastically between the World Wars.*'

Level 3   Identifies and describes the impact of one protest.   **[4 marks]**
For example, '*The government changed their policies towards COs drastically between the World Wars because they realised that COs were here to stay...*'

Level 4   Explains more than one specific reason of impact.   **[5–6 marks]**
For example, '*The government changed their policies towards COs drastically between the World Wars because they realised that COs were here to stay, as the numbers of people claiming exemption had increased significantly since the First World War from 16,000 to 60,000...*'

Level 5   Explains more than one specific reason of impact and compares at least two of the protests.   **[7 marks]**

Level 6   As for level 5 but in addition makes informed assessment about the extent of impact of at least two protests.   **[8 marks]**
For example, '*Clashes between anti-poll tax demonstrators and police highlighted issues about police methods which were developed and introduced during the 1980s to deal with mass protests... Evidence about long-term impact of the 7 July bombings have been the introduction of the Terrorist Act of 2006 and discussion about biometric ID cards, which might affect civil liberties...*'

Now plan and write your own answer. Refer to the chart and the simplified mark scheme to help you achieve the full eight marks available for this question.

Swap answers with a partner. Using the mark scheme, see if you can spot when they move into Levels 5–6. First one to spot it wins!

Putting it all together

You have now completed this unit, which has focused on the changing nature of crime. You have also had practice in answering questions designed to prepare you for your exam. Below is an example of one type of exam question, with some hints to help you write a top-scoring answer.

b Study Source A. Does this source prove that crime was caused by alcohol? Use the source and your knowledge to explain your answer. **[5 marks]**

Source A

Drunkenness, the parent of all other crimes & miseries, the grand [supplier] for her prisons & her workhouses! That the love of drink is widespread & powerful amongst the manufacturers is obvious to everyone... how many victims it loads to a jail. As the object of this letter is to account for the increase of crime, & as a large portion of that increase should, in my opinion, be referred to the prevalence of Drunkenness...

Extract from W. Meyrick's Home Office memo on criminal justice and the causes of the increase in crime, 1828.

What should I write about?	Exemplar answer	Structure and tips
Step 1 Start by annotating the source and write down your initial thoughts. Then pick out one or two things from the source and make a comment from your own knowledge.	For example, *'Meyrick is correct as alcohol did contribute to some of the misery, particularly in inner-city London.'*	This answer provides a good starting point but needs to be developed and not only give general comments.
Step 2 The key to a good answer for this question is to use the source to explain that alcohol was or was not a factor in causing crime.	For example Meyrick says, *'The love of drink... leads [victims] to a jail.'* This suggests a direct link between alcohol and crime. He even states that *'a large portion of that increase'* in crime should be blamed on drink. Therefore, Source A clearly shows the importance of alcohol for increasing crime.	This answer is coming along well but can still be tweaked. When you write, try to make your answer flow better by using connectives to link your writing together. Also, think about the big factors, which contributed to the rise in crime.
Step 3 Even if it is a small question, try to conclude at the end so that the examiner sees that you have considered the question and made a **judgement**.	For example, *'Meyrick was not alone in believing that "drunkenness" was a key reason that crime increased. However, England experienced population increase as well as a shift from rural to urban areas both of which contributed to the steady rise in crime, particularly petty theft, which was one of the most common crimes of the 1800s. Also, wider issues such as the ending of the Napoleonic War in 1815 created many problems when soldiers returned home to find themselves unemployed and poor.'*	A very good answer. The candidate has shown clear contextual knowledge of the 19th century and has explained the impact of a number of different factors.

Fact file

In the exam, you will be asked to answer two questions from Section A, the Development Study: a source-based question and a structured question. The source-based question is divided into three parts – **a**, **b** and **c**. In this Grade Studio we will be looking at how to produce a top-level answer for the type of question that will assess your understanding of the key concepts in this course and your ability to analyse source material, as well as using your contextual knowledge to draw conclusions. Each source question has 5 marks.

Simplified mark scheme

Level 1 Uses source to argue it was/was not the main cause. **[1–2 marks]**
These answers will be restricted to information in the source.
For example, *This source does not prove it was the main cause because Meyrick only mentions problems with prisons.*
or
Evaluates source because of date/secondary

Level 2 Uses source to argue that it was and it was not a failure. **[3 marks]**
These answers will be restricted to information in the source, similar to Level 1 but with a little more detail.

Level 3 Contextual knowledge used to argue that it was/was not a failure. **[4 marks]**
For example, *This source does not prove it was the main cause because Meyrick only mentions problems with overcrowding in prisons. However, Meyrick is correct to an extent, as alcohol was considered by many to have had some impact. Nevertheless, it does not explain that rising population and increased poverty, especially after the end of the Napoleonic Wars when hundreds of thousands of soldiers returned home, was perhaps a bigger reason why crime increased.*

Level 4 Contextual knowledge used to argue that it was and it was not a failure, similar to **[5 marks]**
Level 3 but with a couple more examples.

Now plan and write your own answer. Refer to the chart and the simplified mark scheme to help you achieve the full five marks available for this question.

3.1 Punishment: Four eras of 'vicious punishments'?

GETTING STARTED

Think about the following questions.

1 Should Britain bring back the death penalty for serious crimes?

2 What are the main arguments for and against?

3 How might the information in this lesson be used in a debate about the death penalty?

By the 1950s and 1960s few people were actually getting hanged. Six attempts had already been made to abolish the death penalty altogether, but they had all failed by increasingly narrow margins. However, when the decision was finally taken in 1965, the nation was still divided and at first it was done on a trial basis.

SOURCE

It's of a great adventure to you that I will tell
Of how they hanged a silly boy and how it all befell:
 It was guns and comics, films of war that made his
  education.
Young Craig and Derek Bentley, they went out in the
 night
With gun and knuckleduster just for to see them right:
 It was guns and comics, films of war that made their
  education.
They climbed up on the roof so high and then looked all
 around
And there they saw the men of law all gathered on the
 ground:
 It was guns and comics, films of war that made their
  education.
Look out, we're caught, young Bentley cried, our robbing
 days are done
I'll see no prison, Craig replied, while I've still got my gun:
 It was guns and comics, films of war that made his
  education.
He stood up on the roof so high and then looked all
 around
And he shouted to the men of law all gathered on the
 ground:
 It was guns and comics, films of war that made his
  education.
Stay down and stay alive he cried, keep clear of me he said
Come up that step another step and you'll go down it
 dead:
 It was guns and comics, films of war that made his
  education.

He was a silly, frightened boy who couldn't read or write
But standing there with gun in hand he terrorised the
 night:
 It was guns and comics, films of war that made his
  education.
The men came up to take him down, he pressed the
 trigger tight
He shot the first dead and then jumped down into the
 night:
 It was guns and comics, films of war that made his
  education.
Now Craig he was a killer, for he shot the p'liceman dead
But they couldn't hang a boy so young the hanging judge
 he said:
 It was guns and comics, films of war that made his
  education.
But nine o'clock one Wednesday they took young Bentley
 out
And they made a noose of hempen rope and put it round
 his throat:
 It was guns and comics, films of war that made his
  education.
It's true as you have often heard that in this land today
They hang the little criminals and let the big go free:
 It was guns and comics, films of war that made his
  education.

Lyrics from a 1960s song, written by Karl Dallas about the Derek Bentley case.

The murder conviction of Derek Bentley, the teenager hanged more than 45 years ago for the shooting of a police officer, was quashed yesterday in a historic judgement greeted with tears and elation by his relatives.

Bentley was found guilty of murder in 1952 and hanged in January of the following year, despite the fact that it was his accomplice, Christopher Craig, who fired the fatal shot that killed PC Sidney Miles.

The pair had mounted a break-in at a confectionery warehouse in Croydon, south London, and were cornered by officers on the roof of the building.

Officers told his trial that, immediately before the murder, Bentley had shouted: 'Let him have it, Chris.' The prosecution alleged that, in saying this, Bentley had encouraged Craig to shoot and was therefore equally guilty of the murder. Bentley was hanged at Wandsworth in January 1953. At 16, Craig was too young to hang and was detained at Her Majesty's pleasure for 10 years.

In 1993, Iris Bentley won a partial victory when the then Home Secretary, Michael Howard, granted a limited posthumous pardon, accepting that her brother should not have been hanged.

Report from the *Daily Telegraph*, Friday 31 July 1998, written by Sally Pook.

ACTIVITIES

1 Complete a table like the one here to help you analyse Source A.

2 Using the evidence in the boxes, piece together the story of Derek Bentley.

   Which parts of the story support Source A and which contradict it?

3 Why do you think that the Derek Bentley case convinced more people that capital punishment should stop?

Looking for...	Line from the song...	What it means...
The crime committed		
Bentley's character		
Bentley's mental state		
Bentley's background		
Bentley's punishment		
Christopher Craig's punishment		
Comments on British Justice system		

HISTORY DETECTIVE

Investigate the case of Ruth Ellis. Why might her story have added to the pressure to end the death penalty?

Derek Bentley was not carrying a gun and was being restrained by a police officer when the shooting took place.

Supporters collected thousands of signatures to protest against the death sentence verdict.

The police officer asked Craig to give up his weapon. Craig refused and then Bentley shouted, 'Let him have it Chris!'

The jury in the case recommended mercy for Bentley.

Christopher Craig was only 16 when the incident took place.

Bentley lost an appeal against the verdict and his sentence.

In his police statement, Bentley said, 'I knew we were going to break into the place, I did not know what we were going to get – just anything that was going. I did not have a gun and I did not know Chris had one until he shot. I now know that the policeman in uniform is dead.'

Bentley had already been convicted for petty crime and sent to an approved school.

Bentley was epileptic and had the mental age of an 11 year old.

In 1952 the age of criminal responsibility was 18.

Bentley's former teacher, Hugh Mow, said that Derek was not a violent person. He could not read or write, but his behaviour was normal.

3.2 How important was wealth in deciding punishment for people in Rome?

LEARNING OBJECTIVES

In this lesson you will:

- learn how effective punishments were in Ancient Rome
- compare and contrast a range of factors.

KEY WORDS

Blood money – *payment made to a victim's family after a murder.*

Orator – *someone to speak in court for the defendant.*

Vendetta – *taking revenge over a long period for a previous act.*

GETTING STARTED

In 2007, Paris Hilton was arrested and convicted for driving offences. However, she only spent a total of three days in prison.

Why is it that she spent less time inside than most people could expect for some similar offences?

Is this a fair situation?

The Romans did not have a regular police force, or the money and resources to set one up. Without the fear of getting caught, people would commit crime unless the authorities found a different way to make them respect the law.

The 'Big Idea' that organised Roman punishment was to be really harsh with those who broke the law in order to deter others from doing so. As you saw on page 5 the Romans set down the Twelve Tables and Justinian revised the law to make sure that everyone understood what was a crime and the consequences of breaking the law. Emperors wanted to ensure that society was well ruled and the people were happy, but if this meant being tough then they would do it. In fact, punishments became more violent as time went on.

If everything in the last paragraph was true then everyone should have been treated equally.

Rulers and politicians

The Emperor Julius Caesar was murdered in 44 BCE by around 60 people in the Senate. Despite the numbers involved, no one came forward with information about the culprits and so no action could be taken. The death of the Emperor went unpunished.

Nobles

Most murders were settled privately through the payment of '**blood money**', so it obviously helped to be rich in this case. Many of the nobles employed their own groups of thugs to protect their interests. They were also useful for carrying out **vendettas** against others. Some reprisals carried on for decades and the original feud was forgotten.

If you did end up in court, like the noble Titus Milo in 50 BCE, it was in your interests to hire an **orator** to speak for you. They could present your case in a sophisticated way and enhance your chances of leaving court a free man. Titus Milo employed an extremely famous orator called Cicero. However, he was still found guilty of using his thugs to murder an opponent. He decided to go into exile and lose his land rather than face the death penalty – the usual punishment for murder.

ACTIVITIES

1 Your task is to read the following information and decide whether the rich got a better deal when it came to punishment. Did money spare you from the worst punishments?

2 Find four examples of how wealth made a difference to the punishments given.

3 Which do you think made the most difference to your punishment: wealth, religion or being conquered? Rank order these three factors and explain your choices.

Legionaries

The Roman army had very strict discipline and could inflict serious punishment on its soldiers. The harshest punishment was for deserting your post in battle. Once a deserter was captured, lots were drawn among the legion and one in ten of the soldiers had to die alongside the runaway. The Romans relied on their army and wanted to show soldiers that lack of discipline had serious consequences.

Ordinary Roman citizens

Roman citizens could face the death penalty for a number of crimes including arson, robbing and stealing and most serious of all, attacking the emperor. Market traders and craftsmen might face a whipping or get a fine for selling poor quality goods or trying to con a customer by selling products like bread under weight. Like nobles, they might lose their property, but this did not mean that the other punishments were suspended. In fact, it was likely that they would be executed and lose their property. If criminals were ordered to pay a fine but did not have the money to do so, then they might have to become slaves or enter the gladiator arena to do battle with other wrongdoers.

Slaves

Slaves had few rights and faced some of the harshest punishments. In the 1st century CE, a noble planned to kill all 400 of his slaves, because one of them had attempted to murder him. This caused a riot in Rome, as the people thought this excessive. However, the Emperor Claudius intervened and made sure that the executions went ahead – it was the privilege of nobles to punish slaves in this way. The rich and the rulers were afraid that if slaves did not receive harsh treatment for rebelling then many more would try to overthrow their masters. Despite this, slaves were allowed to speak in court, but only after they had been severely tortured.

Punishment for religious reasons

Christians were mostly crucified for their beliefs in the earlier part of the Roman period. However, as emperors began to adopt the Christian religion, Jewish people

By now, you should have a good understanding of punishment in Ancient Rome. This exercise will help you to plan out and write a top quality answer for the following exam question:

a Briefly describe ways in which the Romans punished criminals. **[5 marks]**

Examiner's tip

Questions that ask you to describe something always contain the word 'describe' and are therefore easy to spot! For this type of question, there are two main aspects to think about:

- Always describe at least three examples.
- Avoid general points and make specific references to the time period.

came under attack. When some Jewish people rebelled, 1 million were killed and several thousand were sent to arenas to die in gladiator games.

Conquered peoples

Do you remember 'Story 4: Massacre in Spain' where the governor of Spain massacred the Lusitanians (see page 44)? Even though it was discussed in Rome, no action was taken. The provinces were governed by whatever means were necessary. Similar events happened in Gaul and in Britain under the Romans.

Conquered people were given great privileges, like a share of power and their own customs, as long as they remained loyal to the Roman Empire, paid taxes and helped man the army. Failure to do these things could result in harsh punishment. In 146 CE Carthage was destroyed completely by flames, because it held out against the Romans. In Africa, disloyal cities had their lands confiscated and had to pay fines. Across the Empire, anyone who refused to fight in the army was made into slave labour.

3.3 Boudica and the Iceni: What was the Roman response to rebellion?

LEARNING OBJECTIVES

In this lesson you will:
- learn about rebellion against Roman rule in Britain
- use information to assess the impact of a historical event.

The Boudican revolt

The Romans conquered a vast empire and their army developed a fearsome reputation for fighting efficiently and winning. So, why did several British tribes try to take them on? What would lead them to do this?

After the death of her husband, Prasutagus, in 60 CE the Iceni lands were left jointly to their daughters and Emperor Nero. This was standard practice in the conquered lands. Boudica was to govern until the girls were old enough to rule, but this was unacceptable to the Roman authorities. They refused to recognise a woman as a legitimate ruler of a conquered state and so a few minor officials organised to seize her land and riches, rape her daughters and flog Boudica.

Tacitus says that Boudica then united all the Britons against the Roman rulers, claiming '… the Britons make no distinction of sex in their appointment of commanders'. It is unlikely to be true, but Boudica did bring together some of the eastern and southern tribes. They found their chance to attack in 61 CE when the governor of Britain, Suetonius Paullinus, had gone to destroy the Welsh island of Anglesey, because he believed the Druids who lived there were encouraging the Celts to rebel. Boudica led the destruction of Colchester, St Albans and London.

Having done this, she went north in pursuit of Paulinus. The two sides met and, after fighting for an entire day, the Romans launched a successful counter-attack and killed thousands of Boudica's warriors. She took poison rather than be captured.

ACTIVITIES

1 Create a list of all the wrongs mentioned that were done both before and during the rebellion.
2 Split the list into those wrongs committed by the Romans and those by the Britons.
3 Who do you think acted worse? Why? Take a class vote to see what others think.

SOURCE

His kingdom was plundered by centurions, his house by slaves, as if they were the spoils of war. First, his wife Boudica was scourged, and his daughters outraged. All the chief men of the Iceni, as if Rome had received the whole country as a gift, were stripped of their ancestral possessions, and the king's relatives were made slaves.

Tacitus *Annals Book 14* on the Romans actions towards the Iceni after the death of the king, Prasutagus.

SOURCE

About seventy thousand citizens and allies, it appeared, fell. For it was not on making prisoners and selling them, or on any of the barter of war, that the enemy was bent, but on slaughter, on the gibbet, the fire and the cross.

Tacitus *Annals Book 14* on the destruction of Colchester, St Albans and London.

The aftermath

The Romans were not slow to respond to Boudica's defeat and death. They sent 7000 additional troops over from Germany to replace losses and reinforce their military presence in Britain. With the arrival of these extra troops, Paullinus was quick to punish the British, even those tribes that had apparently remained neutral.

However, after this initial backlash there seems to have been some political quarrel amongst the Romans that led to Paullinus being recalled to Rome to be replaced by Petronius Turpilianus. This new governor was to follow a more conciliatory tone with the British tribes, although this was not approved of by everyone.

However, the driving force behind the removal of Paullinus was the new Procurator, Julius Classicianus. One of his main responsibilities was the financial governance and taxation of the province of Britain, and continued harsh punishments could only have led to less tax coming into the Imperial treasury.

SOURCE C

Whatever tribes still wavered or were hostile were ravaged with fire and sword. Nothing however distressed the enemy so much as famine, for they had been careless about sowing corn, people of every age having gone to the war.

Tacitus *Annals Book 14.*

SOURCE D

Petronius neither challenged the enemy nor was himself molested, and veiled this tame inaction under the honourable name of peace.

Tacitus *Annals Book 14.*

SOURCE E

The advent of Turpilianus signalled a new attitude towards Britain. Further military action was to cease: no more conquests, no more revenge; reconciliation was to be the order of the day, tact and diplomacy needed to calm British chiefs and introduce the new [Roman] way of life.

Extract from *Boudica*, **written by historian Graham Webster in 1993.**

SOURCE F

A 19th-century portrayal of Boudica.

ACTIVITIES

4. Using the information from this page, complete a table like the one below:

Roman response	Positive or negative effect

5. 'Boudica's revolt failed to free Britain from Roman rule and therefore achieved nothing.' Using the information from this lesson, how far do you agree with this statement?

HISTORY DETECTIVE

Another woman who ruled in Britain at the same time as Boudica was Cartimandua of the Brigantes tribe. Research her life and rule and list the similarities and differences between her and Boudica.

3.4 What factors led to changes in Saxon and medieval punishment?

In the early part of the Saxon era, kings and rulers paid little attention to the punishment of crimes. Most of the work was left to individuals or the tithings. Kings only got involved if crime involved a man without family. However, by the 10th century, as we have seen (pages 9–11), Saxon kings were making complex laws and detailing the punishments given in each case.

Warrior society

A popular way of settling disputes about murder was for the family of the murdered person to attack those responsible for the murder in revenge. This was known as a 'blood feud'. The Saxon system had its origins in warrior society and this meant there was a strong tradition of defending your family and supporters. This was gradually reduced by kings who saw that a continual battle between two families could never bring about peace and would lead to further murders and trouble.

Christian beginnings

One of the main reasons for a move away from the blood feud was the influence of the Church. Bishops were showing rulers that persuading people to repent of their sins and come to God had a much more powerful effect than the simple threat of execution. Under this tutorship Saxon rulers sought for new ways to deal with criminals.

What's it worth?

One system used to control blood feuds was *Wergeld*. This put a price on people's heads that had to be paid if they were murderers.

The fees set down in the 'Laws of Ine' were:
- noble – 1200 shillings
- lesser noble – 600 shillings
- ceorl (free peasant) – 200 shillings
- slave – 60 shillings
- Welshman – no payment

A similar scale can be found for individual body parts in the laws of Ethelbert. Fines were the most popular form of punishment by the 10th century and created a more stable society. However, if people could not pay the fines they were given then the person involved could be made a slave.

Most of these decisions were taken in a court, whose job it was to uphold the law and regulate compensation. Repeat offenders of petty crimes could find themselves being mutilated: hands and feet were cut off for theft, tongues for slander and sometimes eyes were put out.

Ways to die

Despite the fact that many crimes were now punished by fines, there were still some that carried the death penalty. These included treason, treachery against the lord, some murders, arson and house-breaking. Not only were criminals executed, but lost their lands, making their families poor or destitute. There were a number of methods used for death. Hanging was the most popular, but burning, drowning and beheading were also used.

Where am I?

In Saxon times it really mattered where you lived. Due to the fact that England had once been a series of kingdoms, each carried out punishment in different ways. The 10th-century rulers made few attempts to change this and allowed the people in charge of the regions to continue with local customs. In this way they hoped to keep their support.

ACTIVITIES

1 Look at the information about Anglo-Saxon and medieval England and why punishments changed. Your task is to work out why these changes occurred. There are four factors for you to investigate.
   - Money and wealth
   - Religion
   - Conquest, land and people
   - Maintaining a stable society

2 In the previous two lessons, you studied the Roman punishment systems and were asked whether wealth, religion or being conquered was the most important factor in deciding punishment. Now compare medieval, Saxon and Roman times. Was punishment affected by the same three factors but in different ways? Was a different factor more important in Saxon and medieval times? Write down your thoughts.

Case study: Conisbrough Manorial Court

The Manorial Court was the lowest of the courts and was used by the lord of the manor to try those people who lived on his land and had committed offences. The court was supposed to meet every three weeks, but in reality it happened less frequently. In most places, the lord appointed a Steward to run the court in his name. He would be assisted by the bailiffs, and constables. The Steward ran the court, but the jury of twelve men made the decision about guilt. Unless the accused and the victim made an agreement before the trial, an 'inquisition' was held and then the jury would decide on guilt and impose a sentence according to the laws or customs of the area. The Steward could only intervene if he felt that the decision would damage the interests of the lord. Most of the business of the court revolved around land and rent – not surprising, since it was the court of the local lord and his interests would always come first.

Other medieval punishments for ordinary people

As you can clearly see from the records above, the most common punishment was fines. However, other punishments were used to humiliate individuals who had committed petty crimes – usually ones that affected the local community. Public punishments allowed neighbours and acquaintances to see who was committing crimes. These punishments included being put in the stocks, being placed in ducking stools and plunged into water and being whipped.

SOURCE A

Fined for assault: Thomas de Edelington drew blood from Joan de Ullay.

Richard Glede for cutting wood (6d).

Fined for non-attendance: John Maresshal (2d).

Fined for brewing ale without a licence: Joan White (6d), the wife of William Elison and Richard Elisson (4d each).

Fined for assault: Robert Hede drew blood from Walter Nauteherd (2s). William de Waddem rightly raised a hue and cry against Robert Hede who was fined 6d. Total fines 3s 10d.

Fined for [jury] non-attendance: John de Wolde, Nicholas Hudson and Robert Mirfin (6d each); Fined for obstruction of a watercourse: John Custson obstruction at his gates (2d), Robert Hede at Brodegate so that the road deteriorated (12d).

Court records from Conisbrough Manor, 1380.

More serious was theft. Anyone convicted of stealing a shilling or more could be hanged. Minor theft carried a penalty of hands or ears being cut off, being branded with hot irons, or a day in the stocks. These measures did not really deter people; there is evidence to show that 74 per cent of all crimes in the first half of the 14th century were theft.

ACTIVITIES

3 Source A shows some of the Court records for Conisbrough near Doncaster in the 1300s. Do you think the punishments fit the crimes? It will be useful to know that 12d (pence) or 1s (shilling) would be worth about £23 today.

4 Complete a grid like the one below to help organise your work

Crime	Punishment	Fair?
Not attending for Jury duty	Fine of 12d (£23 today)	

The medieval period is often seen as brutal and savage – and this is true of serious crimes like murder and treason. How would an ordinary citizen living in a town like Conisbrough describe the punishment system?

5 Think of three words they might use to describe the system.

6 Use evidence from the court records and your own knowledge to explain why you chose these words.

3.5 Why did medieval kings take a great interest in punishment?

LEARNING OBJECTIVES

In this lesson you will:
- understand how the nature of punishment changed during the Middle Ages
- build up evidence to support a range of factors and come to conclusions.

Punishment of criminals was not simply left to judges and courts in the medieval period. The king had a vested interest in the dispensation of justice, but often for several different reasons. In fact many of the symbols of royalty that were used at coronations were symbols of the king's role in justice. The orb symbolised the king's just and fair rule and the sceptre symbolised a rod to beat and punish wrongdoers.

On this page are four tag team wrestling groups. Each has two wrestlers and supports a cause.

- The Bible Bashers – follow the Christian example.
- The Even Stevens – keep society stable
- The Executioners – deter criminals through fear.
- The Goldiggaz – increase the wealth of the king.

The Bible Bashers

Steven Local

The Even Stevens

ACTIVITY

1. Your task is to read about the special moves and assign them to the team that goes with them. You will need to read each of the moves carefully as they could be used by more than one wrestling team.

1 Warrior choke hold
Medieval kings wanted to end *blood feuds* because too many valuable citizens were being killed. They replaced them with compensation for victims and took a slice of the payment themselves.

2 The corporal boot
There was a move from *Wergeld* to more diverse punishments. Kings wanted to show a deterrent and teach people a lesson for the God-ordained state. Corporal punishment was good for this, because people had to bare the physical pain.

3 Cross of pain
The crown was happy to join forces with the Church. Physical punishments like whipping or branding could work alongside the promise of Hell for those who sinned by committing crime.

4 Gaol house rock

The growth of trade and the crimes that went with it (like getting into debt) needed new punishments. The Church had used gaol for a long time and the state adopted it as a punishment for manufacturing offences and activities that disrupted the public order.

6 The gut wrencher

Treason was a still a serious crime. The Earl of Carlisle was convicted of this crime in the 14th century and he had his bowels and entrails torn out, because that was 'whence came your traitorous thoughts'.

7 The multi-punch

Kings used a variety of punishments such as hanging, flogging, branding, blinding, amputation and outlawry.

8 The ball breaker

In 1125 the king decided to cut the testicles and right hand off all money lenders, after suspicion that they had attempted to alter and cut down the coinage of the land.

9 The money shaker

The number of crimes increased greatly in the medieval period, but judges more often than not gave out fines rather than the physical punishments set down by the law.

10 Local yokel

Local officials were allowed to keep their own customs, which meant that the law was not completely centralised. For example, murderers in Dover were flung from the white cliffs, and in some coastal towns people were tied to a rock and left to drown when the tide came in.

11 Walk of shame

Executions, the stocks and pillories were set up in public spaces to embarrass and shame the victim. Everyone in the local community would see who had committed a criminal act. This was done to deter others.

The Executioners

The Golddiggaz

5 The 4d dangle

The Abbot of Evesham executed someone over the theft of goods worth 4d. So, in 1279 the law was changed so that no one could be executed for less than 12d of theft.

ACTIVITIES

2 Give all the wrestlers an appropriate name. It must give a clue to the evidence that backs up their topic. For example, one of the 'Even Stevens' is called Steven Local, because allowing local differences was one way that kings kept society even and stable.

3 Which factor do you think was the most important in changing punishment?

3.6 Was justice the same for all in the medieval period?

LEARNING OBJECTIVES

In this lesson you will:

- examine court records to uncover aspects of medieval justice
- compare and contrast sources to reach a conclusion.

ACTIVITY

1 Read through Sources A–G and complete a table like the one below:

Crime committed	Who is accused	Judgement

Justice for all

A rhyme about justice that was used in the 14th century said that when it came to medieval justice, the 'poor be hanged by the neck; a rich man by the purse'. This rhyme, which shows the idea that the rich would only be subject to fines, whereas the poor would be more likely to be seriously punished, was one that was believable to medieval audiences. The question that needs to be asked is how accurate a belief it is.

SOURCE A

Jordan, son of Warin, accused Reiner Read, for that he wickedly assaulted him and cutt off his fingers, so that he is maimed. And Reiner comes and defends the assault and says that on a former occasion a concord was made between them, so that [Jordan] remitted him from that appeal for ten marks which [Reiner] paid him.

Records from the court of Shrewsbury in 1171.

SOURCE B

Abraham Wilkinson, and Anthony Mitchell, being apprehended within the liberty of Halifax with nine yards of cloth and two colts [horses]; which cloth we apprise to nine shillings, and the colts to three pounds & forty-eight shillings; all being taken and found with the said prisoners... By the ancient custom and liberty of Halifax the said Abraham Wilkinson and Anthony Mitchell, are to suffer death, by having their heads severed and cut from their bodies.

Extract from court records of 1650 in Halifax. This town had the right to execute criminals who had stolen goods worth 13½ pence from 1280 onwards.

SOURCE C

Jordan, the bishop of Exeter's reeve, was slain at St. Wenn, and on account of his death there fled Reginald Blewin, Edward, Philip, Roland, Odo, and many others, in fact, the whole township. Their chattels were worth fourteen shillings, for which William of Wrotham must answer. All are outlawed at the suit of Jordan's friends.

Records from the court of Shrewsbury in 1171.

SOURCE D

In this year William de Breos the Younger, lord of Brycheiniog, was hanged by the Lord Llywelyn in Gwynedd, after he had been caught in Llywelyn's chamber with the king of England's daughter, Llywelyn's wife.

Extract from the *Chronicle of Ystrad Fflur* from 1230.

SOURCE E

George of Nitheweie appeals Estmar of Netheweye, together with Thomas his son, for assaulting him and wounding him on his arm. And so Thomas is to be arrested. And the jurors say that they well understand that the same Thomas is guilty of the wound. And it is therefore adjudged that there be a duel between them. A day is given to them at Hereford the Wednesday after St. Margaret's Day when they are to appear armed. Thomas was defeated, and blinded and castrated.

Records of the court at Gloucester in 1221.

He was led on foot between the two sheriffs of London from the Tower through the city to Tyburn where he was strangled as common murderers are.

Contemporary account of the hanging of Thomas Fiennes, 9th Baron Dacre in 1541. He was found guilty of the murder of another nobleman's servants whilst poaching.

William Burnell and Luke of the Well are suspected of the burglary at the house of Richard Palmer. Let them purge themselves by water under the Assize.

Records of the Manors of the Abbey of Bec from 1281.

2 Look through your completed chart. Does the evidence above help you answer the following question: *Were the rich able to escape justice during the medieval period?*

3 What other sorts of information might you want to help you fully answer this question?

GradeStudio

By now, you should have a good understanding of medieval punishment in Britain. This exercise will help you to plan out and write a top-level answer for the following exam question:

a Study Source H. Are you surprised that these punishments were used in medieval times? Use the source and your knowledge to explain your answer. **[5 marks]**

Hanging at crossroads for serious offences

Stocks and pillories on the village green for trade offences, debts and drunkenness

Whipping and carting for vagrancy and adultery

Medieval punishments.

Examiner's tip

Questions that ask you if you are surprised about something expect you to agree and disagree with the statement in order to score the top marks. For this type of question, there are two main aspects to think about.

- Always make several points.
- Agree and disagree with the statement.

Below is a table to help you structure your 'are you surprised?' question. Use the guidance in all three columns to help you build your answer. Once you have looked carefully at the question and the table, try to write an answer of your own.

What should I write about?	My answer	Structure and tips
PARAGRAPH 1 Identify any of the punishments and what they were used for, like execution for murder, whipping for petty crimes, crucifixion for religious reasons or fines for selling poor quality goods.	Example: 'No I am not surprised because the punishments used were meant to humiliate. Punishments were public and embarrassing. Due to the fact that there was no police force, they did not want crime to get out of hand and this was a way of using local measures to deal with crime. If stocks and gallows were placed on village greens and crossroads, everyone would see them and being seen by their friends and neighbours should be enough to stop people committing crimes. Embarrassment was the key idea.'	If you make a general point such as 'The Romans killed criminals' you will only get 1 mark. It is enough to explain just one of the punishments at this level or to write about them all generally – what matters is that the punishments were public and designed to embarrass.

3.7 Why was the Bloody Code introduced?

LEARNING OBJECTIVES

In this lesson you will:
- explain why punishment became harder
- demonstrate why the Bloody Code became so widespread.

KEY WORDS

Penal code – *the body of laws relating to crime and punishment.*

The Bloody Code – *the harsh laws that were gradually introduced between 1500 and the 1750s and were punishable by death.*

ACTIVITIES

1 Examine Sources A–C. Why do you think the debate about capital punishment crops up every once in a while?

2 What can you learn from Source B about the difficulties in evaluating evidence about arguments for or against the death penalty?

3 If capital punishment were to be reintroduced and if it included the following crimes, would criminal activity stop?
- Murder
- Theft
- Assault
- Burglary
- Begging

SOURCE A

Polling evidence showed that when the public were asked what would most cut crime, only 6 per cent said sending more offenders to jail was the answer.

The *Guardian*, Tuesday 11 March 2008.

SOURCE B

'The death penalty is a deterrent'. This is not proven. Numerous studies have failed to establish that execution deters better than a long jail sentence. For example, the USA has the highest murder rate in the industrialised world, and rates are highest in southern states where most executions occur.

Amnesty International, 6 February 2007.

SOURCE C

1660s	50 offences
1750	160 offences
1815	288 offences

The rise in the number of offences that could be punished with the death penalty.

In 1688 the English Parliament extended capital punishment to cover a whole series of offences. The Black Act of 1723 increased the number of capital offences by another 50! Previously, punishment by death had only been limited to a very short list of crimes including murder and treason. After the English Civil War and the Glorious Revolution of 1688, the landowning classes (many of whom were MPs) tried to get back some kind of control over the country. The chaos of previous generations, which had been brought about by religious changes and insecurities, social divisions between rich and poor, and bloody civil wars was beginning to come to an end, but a fear of anarchy remained among the ruling elite.

Parliament eventually created the bloodiest **penal code** in Europe, which later became known as **the Bloody Code**. Crimes punishable by death under the Bloody Code included:

- murder
- treason
- damaging Westminster Bridge in London
- stealing goods valued at 5 shillings or more
- highway robbery
- stealing letters
- poaching
- blacking yourself up at night
- impersonating a Chelsea Pensioner
- cutting down young trees
- being in the company of gypsies for a month
- 'strong evidence of malice' in children aged 7–14.

Why did punishments become so bloody?

The Bloody Code did not happen overnight. It took more than 100 years for the long list of crimes to be created and was not a conscious effort to create terror in British society. The reasons are more complicated than that as you can see from the diagram below:

ACTIVITIES

Look at the diagram below.

4 Who wanted a harsher penal code? Why this particular group of people?

5 Why did the list of crimes punishable by death become longer and longer?

6 Why did the Bloody Code eventually disappear? Give reasons for your answer.

Protecting interests

The landowning class emerged as supreme rulers of Britain after the Civil War and conflicts of the 1600s. They were ruling a country of 6.5 million people, most of whom had no political rights at all. They based their power on property ownership, and saw the law's main function as defending their rights and property against other classes, mainly the poor sections of society.

Crime was increasing

The landed elite believed that as towns grew in size and the old village community was beginning to crumble, crime must be on the increase. However, crime was not high and was not increasing.

Printing had been invented in the 1400s and the 17th century saw the introduction of broadsheets and pamphlets on a grand scale. These often told tales of murder and violent crimes. This simply increased the belief that crime was everywhere.

Remove people

The Bloody Code offered a great solution to the crime problem as it got rid of criminals – removal by death. Transportation, which you will study in lesson 3.10, had the same purpose – physical removal of the criminal from Britain to North America or Australia.

Primitive law enforcement

Although measures such as the introduction of thief-takers were attempted, the system of policing remained inefficient until the 1750s. The medieval system of policing did not deter people from crime – something else was needed to do that.

Deter people

It was commonly believed that the harsher the punishment the greater the chance of putting people off criminal activity. Therefore, capital punishments were always carried out in public for all to see (see 'The Idle Apprentice' on page 145). When this did not seem to deter people, new imaginative methods were used to put people off (see lesson 3.9).

3.8 Get your sources sorted!

How successful was the Bloody Code?

LEARNING OBJECTIVES

In this lesson you will:

- understand how the nature of punishment changed during the industrial period
- evaluate a range of factors and explain which are most significant.

GETTING STARTED

Look at the 'Deaths Recorded' statistics for Suffolk in 1805–06 (Source A). Write down five things that you can learn from the source. Try to get points from as many different columns or rows as possible.

As you can see from Source A, the nature of punishment was changing. Although many crimes carried the death penalty, fewer sentences were being carried out than before. There are a number of reasons why this was happening.

Juries and judges were unwilling to convict

By the 1820s, less than 10 per cent of people being convicted of capital offences (carrying the death penalty) were actually being executed. Many judges and juries were not prepared to convict people for minor offences, because they believed the punishment was unfair. As one MP commented in 1770, '… *a man who has picked a pocket of a handkerchief worth thirteen pence is punished with the same severity as if he had murdered a whole family.*' This meant that the system of law and order in Britain was breaking down: no punishment meant no deterrent.

Public executions were no longer effective

Since medieval times, punishments had been in public spaces like the village green so that people would fear them and be ashamed. However, executions were now a day out for families and some brought a picnic. The large crowds meant there was drunkenness and brawling, but it also attracted pickpockets and thieves. In fact, executions were causing the crime statistics to go up.

SOURCE A

Date	Year	Forename	Surname	Age	Crime	Outcome
7 Aug	1805	R	Littlewood alias Smith		Horse stealing	Reprieved
7 Aug	1805	James	Frost		Horse stealing	Reprieved
7 Aug	1805	James	Lucas		Sheep stealing	Reprieved
10 Aug	1805	William	Holmes	46	Rape of a child under 10	Hanged – Ipswich 24 August
2 April	1806	George	Christian	26	Horse stealing	Hanged – Ipswich 12 April
2 April	1806	Shadrack	Dewey	30	Shooting at Captain Brooke	Hanged – Ipswich 12 April
2 April	1806	Dyson	Post		Altering a bank note	Reprieved – transported to Australia for 7 years
2 April	1806	John	Smith		Burglary	Reprieved
2 April	1806	Richard	Fletcher		Stealing 9 watches	Reprieved, 2 years in house of correction
2 April	1806	Benjamin	Colley		Stealing 9 watches	Reprieved, 2 years in house of correction

Death sentences recorded in Suffolk, August 1805–April 1806.

New ideas about punishment were emerging

The Age of Enlightenment, as it became known, brought forward a new way of looking at punishments. The key philosophy was 'experience and experiment'. For punishment, this meant having something that was in proportion to the crime – not hanging people for almost everything. The government had already introduced new punishments so that judges had an alternative to hanging – increasing the chances of a guilty verdict. Transportation was the biggest initiative, but gaols and fines were also being used.

Answering a 'does this prove... ?' question

This exercise will help you to plan out and write a top-level answer for a 'Does this prove...?' question.

b   Study Source B. Does this source prove that punishment in early 19th-century Britain was a failure? Use the source and your knowledge to explain your answer.   **[5 marks]**

How to answer a 'does this prove... ?' question

Step one: read the question, identify and highlight...

- The topic (punishment)
- The time frame (early 19th century)
- The question type (Does this prove...)

Step two: Find some points that agree with the statement.

e.g. 'People like Bentham were criticising the present system so it must have some parts that were not effective.'

Can you find another point?

SOURCE **B**

In most continental nations, though not in Britain... torture was still legal. Enlightenment spokesmen, such as... Bentham in England, condemned all such systems of punishment as inefficient as well as cruel. Bentham advocated lengthy jail sentences instead, during which the felon would work to repay society for his crimes. Kept in his cell in solitary confinement, he was bound to reflect upon his misdeeds, and would hence undergo psychological regeneration.

From Roy Porter, *The Enlightenment*, 2001.

Step three: Add in some of your own knowledge.

Bentham is suggesting reforms such as work and 'solitary confinement'. This suggests that the system was failing, because reform was needed.

e.g. 'Judges and juries were convicting fewer people because...'

Add two more points.

Step four: Find some points that disagree with the statement.

e.g. The Source says that there were problems with torture 'In most continental nations', but not in Britain. This suggests Britain's system was in a better state and shows that it was not a failure.

Back up your points with some of your own knowledge.

This could be used as evidence to support the claim that punishment was not a failure.

3.9 Case study: Which story reveals the most about punishment in the industrial period?

LEARNING OBJECTIVES

In this lesson you will:

- look at and analyse case studies of punishment in industrial Britain
- compare and contrast evidence to assess its value.

William Gibbs, soldier or thief?

In 1802 William Gibbs was sentenced to death for highway robbery. The verdict upset everyone so much they burst into tears, including the judge! Gibbs was a soldier and had served his country well in the Napoleonic Wars and the judge felt that Gibbs was a decent man who had acted out of character and that his crime would be an isolated incident.

Soldiers were given a cash bounty to join up, but often ran out of money and had to try to live by other means. Many turned to crimes like highway robbery.

Gibbs was reprieved and given a prison sentence instead.

GETTING STARTED

Daily Telegraph, 2 Jan 2002

Man is beaten to death chasing car thieves

By Paul Stokes

A MURDER investigation has been launched after a family man was beaten up while trying to stop thieves from taking his in-laws' car.

Kevin Jackson, 31, who has two young sons, gave chase after his wife Julie saw two youths attempting to steal her parents' Toyota from outside his home.

He was subjected to a 'savage and sickening' attack and left for dead in the road near his home in Skircoat Green, Halifax, West Yorkshire, early on Sunday.

Mr Jackson was found with serious head injuries, including a fractured skull, and admitted to intensive care at Huddersfield Royal Infirmary. He never regained consciousness and died, with his wife and family at his hospital bedside, on New Year's Day.

What does this reveal about the country today?

1752	The Murder Act instructs judges to include dissection as part of a death sentence punishment.
1782	A 14-year-old girl is hanged for being in the company of gypsies.
1789	Catherine Murphy becomes the last woman burned at the stake.
1808	Sir Samuel Romilly gets a law passed through Parliament abolishing the death penalty for pickpocketing.
1810	There are still 222 crimes that carry the death penalty.
1816	Four boys between the ages of 9 and 13 were hanged in London for begging.
1820	The Cato Street conspirators become the last people to be beheaded for treason in Britain.
1820–30s	The death penalty is removed from nearly all crimes.
1837	Only treason and murder remain as capital offences.
1868	The last public hanging takes place in Britain, but most counties have already given up the practice.

Important dates in the history of capital punishment.

Margaret Catchpole, sentenced twice

Margaret was born in 1762 and grew up in Brandeston in Suffolk, where she became romantically involved with a smuggler called Will Laud.

Later, she was employed as a servant by the Cobbold family, one of the richest in Suffolk. In 1797, she stole a horse from the Cobbold's stables and rode it to London to sell. The stablekeeper she offered the horse to informed the authorities and she was quickly arrested. At her trial, Elizabeth Cobbold spoke on her behalf and her death sentenced was commuted to 7 years' transportation.

At this time it could take up to 5 years before convicts were actually transported, so Catchpole was held in Ipswich Gaol. In 1800 she escaped and tried to flee the country with her lover, Will Laud. They were caught on a beach not far from Ipswich, and Laud was killed in the struggle.

Catchpole was eventually sent to Australia where she died in 1819.

The Cato Street conspiracy

Influenced by the French Revolution and radical writings, Arthur Thistlewood planned to kill the leading politicians of England and seize power.

In 1820 he set up a plan to storm in and kill members of the Cabinet while they were at dinner. However, a police spy had joined their ranks and before they were able to carry out the attack Bow Street Runners stormed their hideout in Cato Street. After a pitched battle and the death of one of the Runners, Thistlewood escaped with 20 men.

He was arrested the next day, sentenced for murder and treason and then hanged and decapitated.

SOURCE A

The Cato Street Conspiracy by George Cruikshank.

James Rutterford – the man they could not hang

Poaching was a huge problem in the rural areas in the 19th century, especially on large estates. In December 1869, two poachers called James Rutterford and David Heffer set out to poach some game. On their way, they were stopped by an 18-year-old gamekeeper, James Hight. During the confrontation, Rutterford beat the young man with the barrel of his gun and killed him.

The body was discovered 24 hours later and the poachers were easily tracked.

At Hight's inquest Heffer decided to testify against Rutterford. For this, Heffer was released and Rutterford was sentenced to be hanged.

Public hanging had been abolished the year before, so Rutterford would be the first man in Suffolk to hang in gaol. However, many people were now pressing for a complete end to executions. This may have affected those in charge of Rutterford's hanging, because what happened next was bizarre. Just 36 hours before he was due to hang, the doctor and executioner announced that it was '*unsafe*' to execute him because his neck was deformed. They said this might lead to a failed hanging. His sentence was therefore changed to life imprisonment.

ACTIVITIES

1 Look at the four stories of punishment in this lesson. What does each reveal about punishment in Britain? Do they show that things were changing over time?

   Complete a chart for each case that includes the following information:
   • Year
   • Crime
   • Sentence
   • What it reveals about punishment
   • Was punishment changing? Why?

2 Which of the stories do you find most surprising? Why?

3 Apart from the issue of changing punishment, what do the stories reveal about the following factors?
   a International effects (war and empire)
   b Economy (wealth and poverty)
   c Power and government.

3.10 Transportation: When was the ship's bust at her happiest?

Transportation

Transportation was introduced as an alternative to hanging (as you learned in the previous two lessons, juries were growing reluctant to convict people for petty crimes). It involved sending people to a penal colony (prison) in another land, miles away from their home. At first, the government used America, but after the Americans won independence from Britain in 1776, Australia was the main destination. The idea was to frighten criminals with the prospect of being sent to a mysterious land, with no understanding of what life might be like once they were there.

Also, voyages were long and harsh, causing deaths along the way. For example, the trip to Australia took eight months and around 1 per cent of people died on the way.

Transportation was used as a punishment from around 1650 until the 1830s.

Why did transportation eventually stop?

As transportation to the North American plantations stopped after the War of Independence in the 1760s, criminals were transported to the newly discovered Australia.

By sending convicts to Australia, the British government could claim the country as part of the Empire before France and other rivals did the same thing. By 1870, when transportation came to an end, 160,000 criminals had been sent to Australia.

1 Imagine that you are a bust at the head of a ship. Your role is to bring luck to the crew and cargo on board as you forge across the oceans, leading the way. What form and appearance would you have? What would be an appropriate and interesting name for you to have?

2 As a ship's bust, what would make you happy and what would make you sad? Make a list of three things for each.

1654 – Transportation to America is first used.

1776 – American War of Independence ends transportation to North America.

1787 – Transportation to Australia begins.

1790s – British increase their presence in Australia.

1790s – The voyage to Australia took 8 months and many convicts died.

1830s – The voyage to Australia took 4 months, 1% of convicts died.

1835 – Transportation cost £500,000 per year and prisons were cheaper.

1851 – Gold was discovered in Australia, leading to a gold rush.

1852 – Thousands of people leave Britain and head for Australia.

1860s – The government of Australia complain that convicts degrade the country.

1868 – Transportation stops and some transportation ships are turned into prison ships (hulks).

Important dates in the history of transportation.

1 Complete the living graph for transportation as if you were the ship's bust. Think carefully about how each event would make you feel and then make a judgement. Remember to write a brief statement to justify your placement of each event.

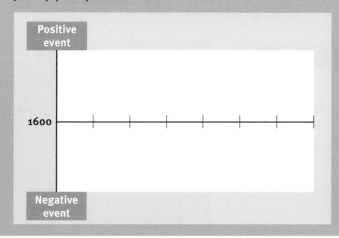

2 Did you find the task easy or difficult? Why do you think you were asked to complete the activity in this way? What other characters could you use to plot the events of transportation?

3 You are in charge of part of a documentary about punishment – your section is on transportation. You are only allowed two minutes of film and you need to make some tough decisions. Create a storyboard for the section – design four frames that will each cover 30 seconds of the documentary. Each frame should look at the following:

- one key event in the history of transportation
- what dialogue will be heard
- what camera and lighting effects will be used
- what song will be used for the soundtrack.

Why were people no longer sent to Australia?

There were a number of factors why transportation to Australia came to an end:

Expensive	Too soft?	Australian's attitudes
By the 1830s transportation was more expensive than imprisonment.	Many people thought that it was more of a holiday than a punishment. When gold was discovered in Australia in 1851, people actually wanted to emigrate.	By the early 1840s people had been transported to Australia for more than 70 years, and settlers set up societies against the 'dumping' of convicts in their country. Australia had become a country in its own right and not everyone was a criminal.
Prison reform	**Decrease in crime?**	**Convicts suffering**
Prisons in England had gone through significant reforms since the 1700s and they were cheaper to run.	Anti-transport champion Sir Molesworth, a member of the House of Commons Select Committee, concluded that transportation did not deter criminals from committing crime.	Several inquiries into the punishment of convicts transported to Australia revealed that many were suffering from the journey and once in the colony.

In the end, the 1853 Penal Servitude Act, which allowed for imprisonment for shorter periods alongside hard labour, meant that only long-term transportation was used and it was finally abolished after the Penal Servitude Act of 1857, although some were still transported after this act. The last transportations took place in 1868.

4 Your school has been invited to take part in a project which teaches primary school pupils about the history of crime and punishment in Britain. Write a report explaining the reasons why transportation ended so that a year 6 pupil (10–11 years old) would understand.

3.11 Case Study: Why did quiet whispering make Tolpuddle a dangerous place to live?

LEARNING OBJECTIVES

In this lesson you will:

- find out about the 'Tolpuddle Martyrs' as a case study why and where transportation was used
- collaborate to solve a history mystery and explain how you solved it

VOICE YOUR OPINION!

Work in groups of three.

- Identify key themes/factors amongst the clues.
- What clues link together?
- Categorise them into groups and explain why the Tolpuddle Martyrs were punished so severely.
- Why would the government in the early 1800s be so afraid of trade unions?

In 1834, six farm workers were arrested in the picturesque village of Tolpuddle, Dorset. They were sentenced to 7 years' transportation to Australia; a very hard sentence. Why did this happen? What had they done to deserve such a harsh punishment?

SOURCE A

George Loveless, one of the six 'Martyrs', in chains at Salisbury, during his journey from Dorchester to a prison hulk, the 'York' at Portsmouth, to await transportation.

1 Below are 24 clues. Use them to solve the mystery – why did quiet whispering make Tolpuddle a dangerous place to live? – and make sure that you can explain how you solved the task.

In 1811, workers, upset by wage reductions, destroyed machines in factories – the Luddite Riots.

The government became suspicious of workers becoming organised, particularly if they met in secret – they could be plotting a revolution! So they ordered local law and order men to take serious action against any union groups.

George Loveless supported his family on a ploughman's wage of 9 shillings a week.

Loveless formed the 'Friendly Society of Agricultural Labourers' in 1834 and made each of the six members swear an oath never to tell anyone about the society and to work towards getting better wages.

Most of the Dorset magistrates were landowners.

The Grand National Consolidated Trades Union (GNCTU) was formed in 1833. Within months the GNCTU had 500,000 members.

If a revolution started in Britain, the country could be vulnerable to foreign invasion.

Employers hated and feared workers' groups and many refused to employ them. Some even sacked workers who belonged to a union.

Since the French Revolution of 1789 the rich people of Britain had been uneasy about large groups of workers.

Loveless' men met in a room and talked in whispers to avoid being overheard. The manor farm they worked at was only a stone's throw away.

The government were becoming very worried by the growing strength of the GNCTU.

Farm wages had been declining for several years in Dorset and by 1834 landowners were threatening to put them down from 10 to 6 shillings a week.

At sea it was illegal to take secret oaths – in case you were plotting against the captain and planning to take over the ship. It was called the Mutiny Act.

Between 1830 and 1832 there were 326 cases of arson and 390 attacks on threshing machines in the Midlands.

Lord Melbourne, the home secretary, told the Dorset magistrates about the Mutiny Act and encouraged them to use it.

Robert Owen formed the GNCTU to fight for better wages and conditions.

In 1825 the government passed a new law that said trade unionists could not 'molest or obstruct' other workers.

The Tolpuddle farmers agreed to join the GNCTU, but decided to keep it secret out of fear that landowners would try to break the union.

After years of war, high taxes, low wages and poor working conditions, farm labourers finally snapped in the 1830s – The Swing Riots.

Most landowners had tried to stop their labourers joining unions and some sacked those who did join.

The government found an old naval law, the Mutiny Act 1797.

The vague wording of the 1825 Act made it possible for courts to prosecute almost anyone who went on strike.

George Loveless and his friends were transported to Australia for 7 years.

It cost around 10–14 shillings a week to lead a normal life.

3.12 How far was the treatment of women and children prisoners improved in the industrial period?

In this lesson you will:

- understand how the punishment of women and children changed between 1800 and 1900
- evaluate evidence and make judgements about its impact.

GETTING STARTED

Look carefully at Source A. It shows Elizabeth Fry, a prison reformer, visiting the female prison at Newgate in 1813. Working in pairs, note down two comments for each square in the grid about what you can learn from this picture.

Fact file

Elizabeth Fry – Born into a Quaker family in Norwich, Elizabeth Fry dedicated her life to helping those less fortunate than herself. After a visit to Newgate Prison, she began a school and Bible group inside the prison in 1817. The following year she gave evidence to a Parliamentary Committee about her work at Newgate.

SOURCE A

Elizabeth Fry at Newgate Prison, 1813.

SOURCE B

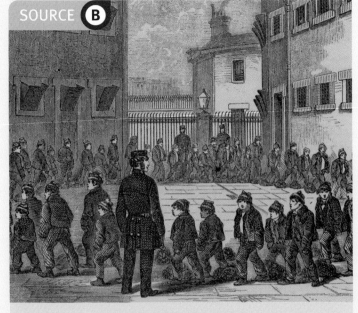

Inside Tothill Prison for the young, 1862.

1 Copy and complete the chart below which shows how punishment towards women and children changed from 1800–1900. For each step, decide whether changes to punishment for women or children is making the most progress and put a tick in the appropriate column. After looking at all the steps, decide who made the most progress by adding up the ticks.

By 1900, all prisons were separated and they dealt with just men, just women or just juveniles.

2 What did you think of the chart below? Was it a fair way to assess progress?

3 Can you suggest three ways to improve the activity to make it a fair comparison?

Treatment of women	Your judgement about progress:		Treatment of children
	women	children	
STEP ONE 1800 – all criminals are kept together			STEP ONE 1800 – all criminals are kept together
STEP TWO 1817 – Elizabeth Fry set up the Improvement of Female Prisoners in Newgate			STEP TWO 1819 – Warwick Gaol creates a separate programme for juvenile offenders
STEP THREE 1820s – Fry's aims of clear rules, education and useful work spread to other prisons			STEP THREE 1838 – Parkhurst was opened, the first prison only for juveniles. There was education, but individuals were separated and kept in solitary confinement
STEP FOUR 1823 – It is compulsory to have female warders looking after women in prison			STEP FOUR 1850 – Reformatory schools were set up. They wanted to steer young people away from crime with a mixture of education, hard labour and punishments
STEP FIVE 1835 – Inspectors are appointed to ensure new rules are followed in prisons and on convict ships			STEP FIVE 1870 and 1901 Education Acts make schooling compulsory and reduce crime levels
STEP SIX 1863 – Brixton Prison was opened. It was the first women-only prison			STEP SIX 1899 – Separate prisons opened for children. The first one was in Borstal in Kent. They become known as *borstals*
TOTAL TICKS:			
Your conclusions:			

3.13 Who was the greatest prison reformer of the 19th century?

ACTIVITY

1 All the profiles of leading prison reformers in this lesson were researched and written by Year 10 students, using textbooks and the internet. Their task was to prove that the person they were investigating was the greatest prison reformer.

   Read each of the following profiles and decide if each of the prison reformers meets the 5Rs of significance.

GETTING STARTED

Can you think of an individual from the last few years who has made a really positive impact on the world (or at least a small part of it)? They do not have to be famous; they just need to have made a positive impact on something.

Does your person fulfil the following criteria?
- Are they remarkable (talked about)?
- Are they remembered by others?
- Does their story reveal something about the world they live in?
- Have their actions had a long-lasting or wider impact on society?
- Have their actions resulted in change?

We call these questions the 5Rs of significance.

Jonas Hanway, 1760s–1780s (by Tom)

A number of individuals put pressure on the government to reform conditions in prisons. The first to suggest a new programme was Jonas Hanway. He believed that prisoners would be rehabilitated by good hygiene and Christian ideas. He wanted separate accommodation for each prisoner and daily visits from a chaplain. Hanway was an influence on John Howard – he led the way for others reforming prisons in the 18th and 19th centuries. Hanway also played a big part in Elizabeth Fry's work: their suggestions are very similar, but he was before her. They both wanted prisoners to take up the Bible and the Christian church. Without him there would have been fewer ideas around about reforming the dreadful prisons.

John Howard, 1777 (by Alice)

One of Howard's jobs was High Sheriff of Bedfordshire and in 1773 he went to inspect the county gaols and he was shocked by what he saw. He made it his life's work to visit and report on every prison. He was extremely careful in his work, measuring each cell, weighing food, noting numbers and type of prisoners and recording deaths from disease. This shows that he got evidence for his reports. His report on England and Wales came out in 1777 showing he was serious about his work. Howard recommended more space, better food, paid gaolers and separation of types and genders of prisoners. Peel was influenced by Howard and put a lot of his work into the 1823 Gaols Act.

Robert Peel, 1823 (by Gemma)

Peel got the Gaol Act through Parliament and made the thoughts of Hanway, Howard and Fry real. The act covered 130 prisons. He made sure that prisons separated women prisoners and they were only looked after by women wardens. His aim was for prisons to be efficient and this meant paying gaolers to do a professional job and JPs had to visit their gaols regularly and report to the quarter sessions and the government. Education, religion and work were adopted to reform prisoners. His work is still talked about today as women prisoners are still separated.

(a) Gaoler – Salary: None
   Chaplain – Salary: £40
   Surgeon – Salary: None

(b) 1 June 1777 Total prisoners: 16 debtors,
   24 criminals

(c) There is only one small day room, twelve feet
   by eleven, for men and women criminals. The
   ward for debtors is nineteen feet by eleven, has
   no window so part of the plaster wall is broken
   down for light and air. The night room for male
   criminals is close and dark and the floor so
   ruinous that it cannot be washed. The whole
   prison is much out of repair.

Extracts from the report on Gloucester Gaol by John Howard,
1777.

George O. Paul, 1780–85 (by David)

In 1780, George O. Paul became High Sheriff of
Gloucestershire. He read Howard's report of 1777
about Gloucester and was disgusted. He asked the
people in charge of Gloucester if he could build a new
prison and in 1785 he was given the power to do it.
He made sure the prisoners were healthy and made
sure they had plenty of fresh air, because he believed
disease was caused by bad air. He had surgeons to
help the sick and visit every prisoner once a week.
Prisoners were made to spend long periods of time on
their own to think about their crimes. Prisoners were
reformed through work, education and religion.
Paul's prison and rules were a model for other
prisons. He also influenced Robert Peel; Peel adopted
and tried to make health education and surgeons
better in the 1823 Gaol Act.

ACTIVITY

2 Now that you have read the case for each of the six
   reformers, it is time to choose the most influential.

   In small groups, consider the issues carefully, then
   award points to each of the six reformers – you
   have 30 points to award in total. The more points
   you give each person, the more influential you think
   they are. Everyone must have at least one point and
   no two people can have the same score. When
   you've finished, share your scores with other
   groups in the class.

Elizabeth Fry, 1813–17 (by Stacey)

She altered the prisons and other people's ideas in
order to improve the standards of prisons for women.
Robert Peel took up many of Fry's ideas in his Gaols
Act in 1823.

Her work was vital for changing prisons, because she
changed female prisons for the better and she
managed to change things when other people failed.
For example, after 1823 women had to have female
gaolers and warders. She wanted to make an
improvement in Newgate in 1817, because of the poor
conditions. She had a belief that prison is a place
from which human beings can emerge better people
than they went in. Her own reforms cost money and
she knew many prisons would not take them up
unless they had to. Elizabeth was disappointed at
how weak the 1823 Gaol Act was. She was the most
influential because her ideas struck a chord abroad,
where women from Paris to St Petersburg formed
prison visiting committees and everywhere she went,
especially in France and Italy, she was welcomed with
respect.

Jeremy Bentham 1820–1830s (by Callum)

In the 21st century, some people think that prisons
are too soft and they should only be there to punish
the criminals. As a result, they reverted back to
Jeremy Bentham's idea of harsh prisons where
criminals learnt their lesson. Jeremy Bentham
believed in architectural designs and a management
scheme to keep prisons in order and well kept.

He also saw that useful work was good for prisoners
and helped them to learn new skills. But most of all
he wanted prisoners to have no contact with each
other, so that they could concentrate on their crimes
and think about how to live a better life. In their cell
they had to work, pray and have religious lessons.
Bentham designed quite a few 'separate system'
prisons.

3.14 Why did prisons need a makeover in the 19th century?

LEARNING OBJECTIVES

In this lesson you will:
- learn about the prison reforms of the 19th century
- understand how change over time can have both positive and negative consequences.

GETTING STARTED

On the BBC website, the home page for DIY SOS reads, 'Is your home more of a DIY disaster zone than a tranquil retreat from the rest of the world?... if you've got a DIY debacle at home, get in touch. Maybe you've had a tough time of it recently and need a miracle to give you a room that would change your life. Or there's been a bodger at work. Whatever the problem, get in touch, DIY SOS is always looking for stories.'

Why do you think people apply to the show?

KEY WORDS

Crank handle – *a useless punishment. Criminals had to turn a handle for most of the day, just to waste their time.*

Gin shop – *a shop selling alcohol (gin was the most popular drink at the time).*

Welcome to our prison makeover! We have been worried for quite some time that these rooms were, quite frankly, rat-infested dirt holes. This is what we found when we had a look around.

SOURCE A

*This home for criminals came with its own **gin shops** – not exactly the strict punishment we were expecting!*

King's Bench prison, 1808.

SOURCE B

The situation in Newgate was even worse. Here, it appeared that the law and justice had completely slipped. No one wants to see scenes like this!

Satirical view of Newgate, 1735.

What new ideas have been introduced?

Here is a cell for one with a **crank handle** that has to be turned 10,000 times a day. The cost might be expensive, but keeping the prisoners separate is clearly the best way to go. It means that they have time to pray and reflect on their crimes.

Prison cell in Surrey, 1851.

ACTIVITY

1   Four systems have been outlined on this page: the separate system, the silent system, useless work and useful work. In the 19th century two major debates emerged about exactly how prisons should punish inmates.

The first debate was between silent and separate systems. Why do you think that silent systems were most widely used? Look for clues on this page.

The second debate was between supporters of useful and useless work. Why do you think that useless work was most widely used? Look for clues on this page.

This is my favourite room. Here I have installed a treadmill, where prisoners can walk forever and get nowhere. Prisons everywhere will want one of these.

Treadmill at Brixton Prison, 1817.

In this room, prisoners are still engaged in useful work, but are allowed contact with each other. The whole atmosphere is one of silence though.

Millbank useful work room, 1862.

VOICE YOUR OPINION!

How much do you think that fear of crime at this time affected punishment?

3.15 Have punishments changed for the better in the 20th century?

PART ONE: Prisons

LEARNING OBJECTIVES

In this lesson you will:
- learn about how controversial prisons are as a form of punishment
- use evidence to support interpretations.

KEY WORDS

Birching – *using a thin piece of wood to beat someone.*

GETTING STARTED

This is an image of Newgate prison in 1900. Based on what you already know, write down five things you would expect to see happening inside the prison.

There are two views about what should happen in prisons and whether it is currently fulfilling its purpose.

Viewpoint 1

Prisons are too soft and do not punish people enough. Why should we expect young people to stay away from crime when they are sure that being caught will result in little more than a telling off?

Even those who commit serious offences are given short sentences – a murderer could be out in 12 years if they behave. Inside they have more luxuries than ordinary working people: TVs, decent food, leisure facilities and entertainment. How can that be fair? We need to get tough on all criminals and we should bring back hanging for murderers and people who commit crimes against children – these people do not deserve to live.

Viewpoint 2

Prison does not work; this has been proved time and time again. More often than not, those who go to prison reoffend after their release and so we need to think about more effective ways of punishing. The idea of going to prison is a powerful one and so we should be looking at short sentences followed by an alternative measure that helps the person rehabilitate. Prisons are already overcrowded and badly run; the last thing we need to do is pile in more prisoners. The State needs to set an example of how to behave; harsh punishments and hanging do not demonstrate a sensible and acceptable response to crime.

Why do you think that Viewpoint 2 has got the most support among politicians at the moment? The public would have more sympathy with Viewpoint 1. Why do you think that is?

ACTIVITY

1 Below is a chart showing some of the measures that have affected prisons in the 20th century. Copy and complete the chart. For each measure, say how it would help to strengthen the case of both viewpoints. Some examples have been added for you.

VOICE YOUR OPINION!

Why do you think that Viewpoint 2 has got the most support among politicians at the moment?

Would the public have more sympathy with Viewpoint 1? Why do you think that is?

To support Viewpoint 1	Changes to prisons in 20th century	To support Viewpoint 2
	1902 – the treadmill and crank were abolished	
	1907 – on release, prisoners were given a probation officer to help them adjust and stay out of prison	
	1914 – offenders were given more time to pay fines	This is sensible and would help to keep people out of prison and playing a useful role in society
	1921 – arrow uniforms and shaven heads were abolished	
	1922 – solitary confinement was ended in prisons	
	1923 – prisoners were given time to talk to each other	
Another example of an 'easy ride'. No one can really call this a punishment	1936 – the first 'open' prison was set up in Wakefield. It had relaxed rules and prisoners were allowed to work outside the prison	
	1945 – more open prisons in operation	
	1948 – flogging and hard labour were ended	
	1948 – the Criminal Justice Act gave prisoners more time to learn new skills and get training. Also, prisoners gained better rights and privileges, like diet and TV	This is the only way to avoid people becoming repeat offenders. They need to see there is a chance to do something worthwhile after prison
	1962 – fines and prison sentences replaced **birching** as a punishment	
	1967 – suspended sentences were introduced to help offenders avoid prison and learn to be part of the community	
	1972 – Community Service Orders were introduced to help rehabilitate people by working in the community that they damaged	
	1980s – more prisons were built to help the government get tough on crime	
	1981 – Leeds prison housed 1200 inmates; it was built for 624	
	1990 – inmates at Strangeways prison in Manchester rioted in protest of poor conditions	
	2008 – prison reform groups bid to take over the running of some prisons	

3.16 Have punishments changed for the better in the 20th century?

PART TWO: Juvenile and alternative punishments

LEARNING OBJECTIVES

In this lesson you will:

- learn about punishment for young people and alternatives to prison over the last 100 years
- begin to understand that historical events should be judged in their context.

KEY WORDS

Contextual knowledge – *knowledge about the period in which an historical event took place.*

Parole – *early release from prison for good behaviour.*

GETTING STARTED

There are three eras of punishment:

Age of *revenge* (for example, use of *blood feud*)
Age of *remove* (for example, use of transportation)
Age of *reform* (for example, use of education in prisons)

Revenge	Remove	Reform
Early Modern Period	Industrial Period	20th century

Look back in the chapter and find three examples of revenge punishments and three examples of remove punishments.

ACTIVITIES

1. At what point did punishment become only about reform?

2. Which of the four eras saw the most significant progress being made (this might not be the same era as the point where the crossover happened)?

3. Look back over this chapter. Try to answer the three questions below:

   a. Why do you think that in the Roman, Saxon and medieval times 'revenge' was the key idea in punishment? Why did society at this time need to have this kind of system?

   b. Why was there a move to 'remove' punishments in the 18th and 19th centuries and not before?

   c. Why is it that 'reform' systems have only been seen as acceptable in the 20th century?

4. Look at the chart opposite. It gives information about juvenile and alternative punishments since 1900. Your task is to decide the exact moment when punishment stopped being about removing people from society and became solely interested in *reforming* the individual. Reforming a person is about making them give up crime and showing them how they can make a useful contribution to society.

   For each measure, make a brief note that explains your thinking at that point, showing what is being achieved and how far things have moved towards 'reform'.

   Two examples have been done for you.

Alternatives to prison	Your notes	Juvenile punishment
Before the First World War (1900–14)		
	This did not mean reform – it just separated out criminals.	1900 – Borstals were set up for juvenile offenders.
1907 – Probation started so that offenders met with officer after release.		
1914 – People given fines as punishment were allowed longer to pay.		
Around the Second World War and its aftermath (1933–48)		
		1933 – The age of criminal responsibility is raised to 8.
		1948 – Detention centres set up and offer short sentences with hard punishment.
The 1960s		
1962 – Birching ended as a punishment.		
		1963 – The age of criminal responsibility raised to 10.
1965 – Capital punishment abolished.		
1967 – **Parole** introduced as an incentive for good behaviour.		
1967 – Suspended sentences introduced to keep people out of prison and in the community.	This was another measure aimed at showing people how to live effectively in the community. It reinforces the idea of reform.	
		1969 – Special courts, supervision and care orders were started.
		1969 – The age of criminal responsibility raised to 14.
Britain in the European Community (1973–2008)		
1972 – Community service started to help people repair damage to the community.		
		1983 – Detention centres and youth custody replaced borstals for under 21s.
1990s – Electronic tagging started.		
		1999 – Anti-Social Behaviour Orders introduced.

HISTORY DETECTIVE

In this exercise, you will investigate how attitudes towards the purpose of punishments developed across time. As you examine the reasons why some punishments appeared and then eventually disappeared write down the reason(s) for this change. Similarly, some punishments may have continued, or may have altered in some way.

This activity has been divided into two parts:

Research, using the book to investigate a number of punishments:

- mutilation
- banishing
- stocks/pillory
- hard labour
- transportation
- community service
- branding
- whipping
- fines
- execution/hanging
- prison
- any others

Create a table like the one on page 131 to use during your research.

3.17 What was the purpose of punishment in the 20th century?

LEARNING OBJECTIVES

In this lesson you will:
- analyse the purpose of punishment
- evaluate evidence and arguments.

GradeStudio

You have just looked at the debate about punishment in the 20th century and should now have a good understanding of how controversial the changes were. You have also been practising a key skill needed to achieve at GCSE: creating opposing arguments. Below is a table that will help you to answer the following question:

c How far were punishments in the 20th century different from those used in earlier periods? Explain your answer.

[8 marks]

What should I write about?	My answer
Introduction Begin by talking about the purpose of prisons – why are they used? Why are they so popular?	For example, '*Prisons are the most widely used punishment in Britain. They are designed to keep dangerous criminals and serial criminals away from the general public. However, over the past 100 years there has been a movement away from using prison as a deterrent and to use it as a place of rehabilitation. The evidence suggests that...*'
PARAGRAPH 1 Set out the case for things that are different. Try to mention: • rehabilitation • less humiliation • alternatives to prison.	For example, '*The main idea that has guided punishment in 20th century is 'rehabilitation'. Slowly, useless punishments like the crank handle were withdrawn and schemes like training for jobs were brought in. This suggests that...*'
PARAGRAPH 2 Build a case for similarities. Try to mention: • variety of punishments • prison/gaol used • overcrowding and violence.	For example, '*Many of the measures in the 20th century, for example the introduction of community service in the 1970s, were designed to offer judges more options for punishment. This would allow them to make the punishment fit the crime. This is no different to the demand for transportation at the time of the Bloody Code in Britain...*'
CONCLUSION What do you think?	For example, '*There are still prisons like those hundreds of years ago, but the purpose of them has changed. The government still lock people away and remove them from society, but now they are treated in a decent way and people try to help them rehabilitate. So overall I do not think the type of punishments have changed, but their purpose certainly has.*'

Examiner's tips

Top-level candidates will do two things:
- explain examples of similarities and differences in their answer
- reach a supported conclusion about 'how far' things have changed.

The KEY PHRASE here is 'how far'. You cannot get top marks unless you specifically say what has changed and **by how much**.

Structure and tips

Make your argument clear right from the start. It makes your writing more organised and the examiner will be more focused on what you want to say.
Write about each of the points and explain how these changes led to other problems.
At the end of your paragraph, create a mini-conclusion by referring back to the question.
Write about each of the points and explain what other factors help to explain why.
At the end of your paragraph, create a mini-conclusion by referring back to the question.
Try to make a judgement.

Type of punishment	Crimes committed	Purpose of punishment	Similarity to other punishments?	What was the current thinking behind this punishment and what *factors* influenced it?

You are now going to evaluate the different purposes of different punishments. Consider these types of purpose:

- remove
- reform
- hurt
- deter
- vengeance
- compensate.

Make a similar living graph to the one below and place each punishment in chronological order on the timeline with an explanation of the purpose of the punishment. If a punishment carried on then draw an arrow along the timeline until the punishment disappeared or changed.

Finally, use your **research** to make a judgement about the **severity** of each type of punishment. The first one has been completed for you.

When you have completed this exercise, do the Grade Studio that follows. By completing both activities you will have:

- evaluated changes in attitudes towards punishment over time
- analysed a source and used your own knowledge to explain the significance of certain punishments.

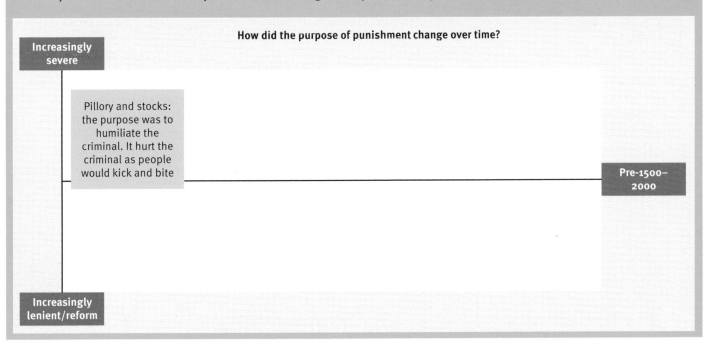

How did the purpose of punishment change over time?

Increasingly severe

Pillory and stocks: the purpose was to humiliate the criminal. It hurt the criminal as people would kick and bite

Pre-1500–2000

Increasingly lenient/reform

Putting it all together

You have now completed this unit, which has focused on the changing nature of punishment. You have also had practice in answering questions designed to prepare you for your exam. Below is an example of one type of exam question, with some hints to help you write a top-scoring answer.

a Study Source A. Are you surprised that these crimes could be punished by the death penalty? Use the source and your knowledge to explain your answer. **[5 marks]**

> **Source A**
>
> *Cutting down growing trees.*
>
> *Being out at night with a blackened face.*
>
> *Stealing from a rabbit warren.*
>
> **A list of some of the crimes that could be punished by the death penalty in the late 18th century.**

Examiner's tip

Before you answer this question, look carefully at the following chart. It gives some of the issues that could be worth thinking about. Then read the candidate's answer. Using the chart and the simplified mark scheme opposite, can you spot why the candidate moved up the levels?

What should I write about?	Exemplar answer	Structure and tips
Step 1 The key to a good answer for this question is to explain the link between the crimes mentioned in the source set against the wider issues of the time period.	For example, *'No I am not surprised because the laws in those days were passed by the landed classes. They wanted to protect their property. They regarded the rabbits on their land as their property and they saw poaching as theft. They did not want people making their faces black because this is what they did when they were poaching at night so they…'*	This answer is coming along well but can still be tweaked. When you write, try to make your answer flow better by using connectives to link your writing together. Also, think about the big factors that contributed to the landed classes enforcing such harsh laws.
Step 2 Even if it is a small question, try to conclude at the end so that the examiner sees that you have considered the question and made a **judgement**.	For example, *'Crimes committed against property were treated particularly harshly **as** the landed classes who created the laws of the country tried to protect their own interests **and** were fearful of **revolution** from the poorer sections of society. **Therefore**, by using harsh punishments the government, which was made up of these men with property, tried to protect their own political positions whilst attempting to cut crime.'*	A very good answer. The candidate has shown clear contextual knowledge of the 18th century and has explained why those particular offences were punished so harshly.

Fact file

In the exam, you will be asked to answer two questions from Section A, the Development Study: a source-based question and a structured question. The source-based question is divided into three parts – **a**, **b** and **c**. In this Grade Studio we will be looking at how to produce a top-level answer for the type of question that will assess your understanding of the key concepts in this course and your ability to analyse source material, as well as using your contextual knowledge to draw conclusions. Each source question has five marks.

Simplified mark scheme

Level 1 Answers based on everyday empathy. **[1 mark]**

> For example, *'Yes, I am surprised. It is quite ridiculous to punish people with death for stealing rabbits. This is far too harsh.'*

Level 2 Assertions of no surprise because punishments at that time were very harsh – no contextual explanation. **[2 marks]**

> For example, *'No I am not surprised because that is what things were like then. They did punish people very harshly.'*

Level 3 Contextual knowledge of the 18th century used to explain why punishments were harsh at that time. **[3–4 marks]**

> For example, *'No I am not surprised because this was the time of the Bloody Code when hundreds of minor crimes were punished by death. This is because people thought the crime rate was going up and something had to be done to stop it.'*

Level 4 Contextual knowledge of the 18th century used to explain why those particular offences were punished so harshly. **[5 marks]**

> For example, *'No I am not surprised because the laws in those days were passed by the landed classes. They wanted to protect their property. They regarded the rabbits on their land as their property and they saw poaching as theft. They did not want people making their faces black because this is what they did when they were poaching at night so they would not be seen.'*

Now plan and write your own answer. Refer to the chart and the simplified mark scheme to help you achieve the full five marks available for this question.

Swap answers with a partner. Using the mark scheme, see if you can spot when they move into Levels 3–4. First one to spot it wins!

Bringing it together

Examining the big picture

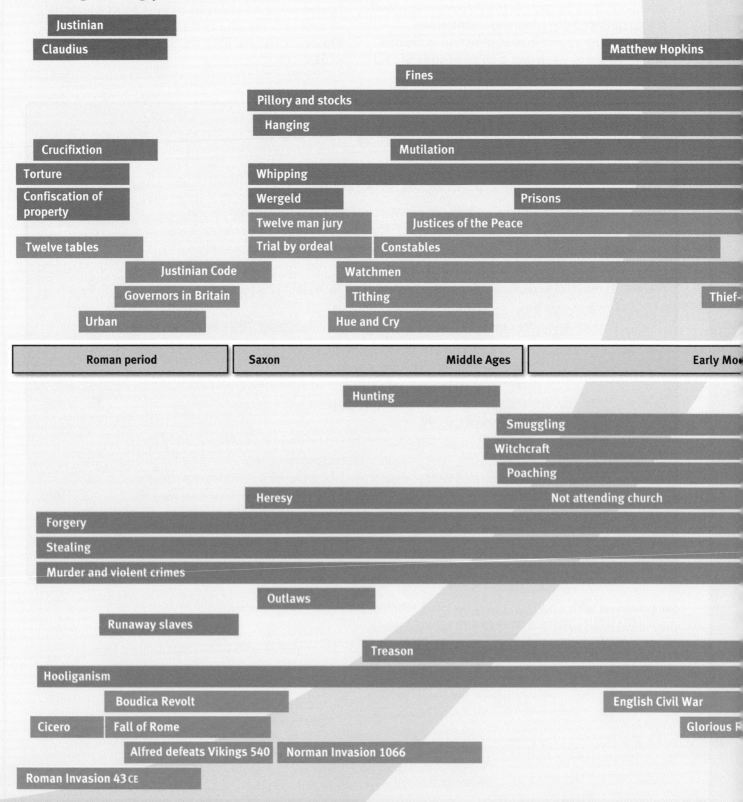

Justinian
Claudius
Matthew Hopkins
Fines
Pillory and stocks
Hanging
Crucifixtion
Mutilation
Torture
Whipping
Confiscation of property
Wergeld
Prisons
Twelve man jury
Justices of the Peace
Twelve tables
Trial by ordeal
Constables
Justinian Code
Watchmen
Governors in Britain
Tithing
Thief-
Urban
Hue and Cry

| Roman period | Saxon | Middle Ages | Early Mo |

Hunting
Smuggling
Witchcraft
Poaching
Heresy
Not attending church
Forgery
Stealing
Murder and violent crimes
Outlaws
Runaway slaves
Treason
Hooliganism
Boudica Revolt
English Civil War
Cicero
Fall of Rome
Glorious R
Alfred defeats Vikings 540
Norman Invasion 1066
Roman Invasion 43 CE

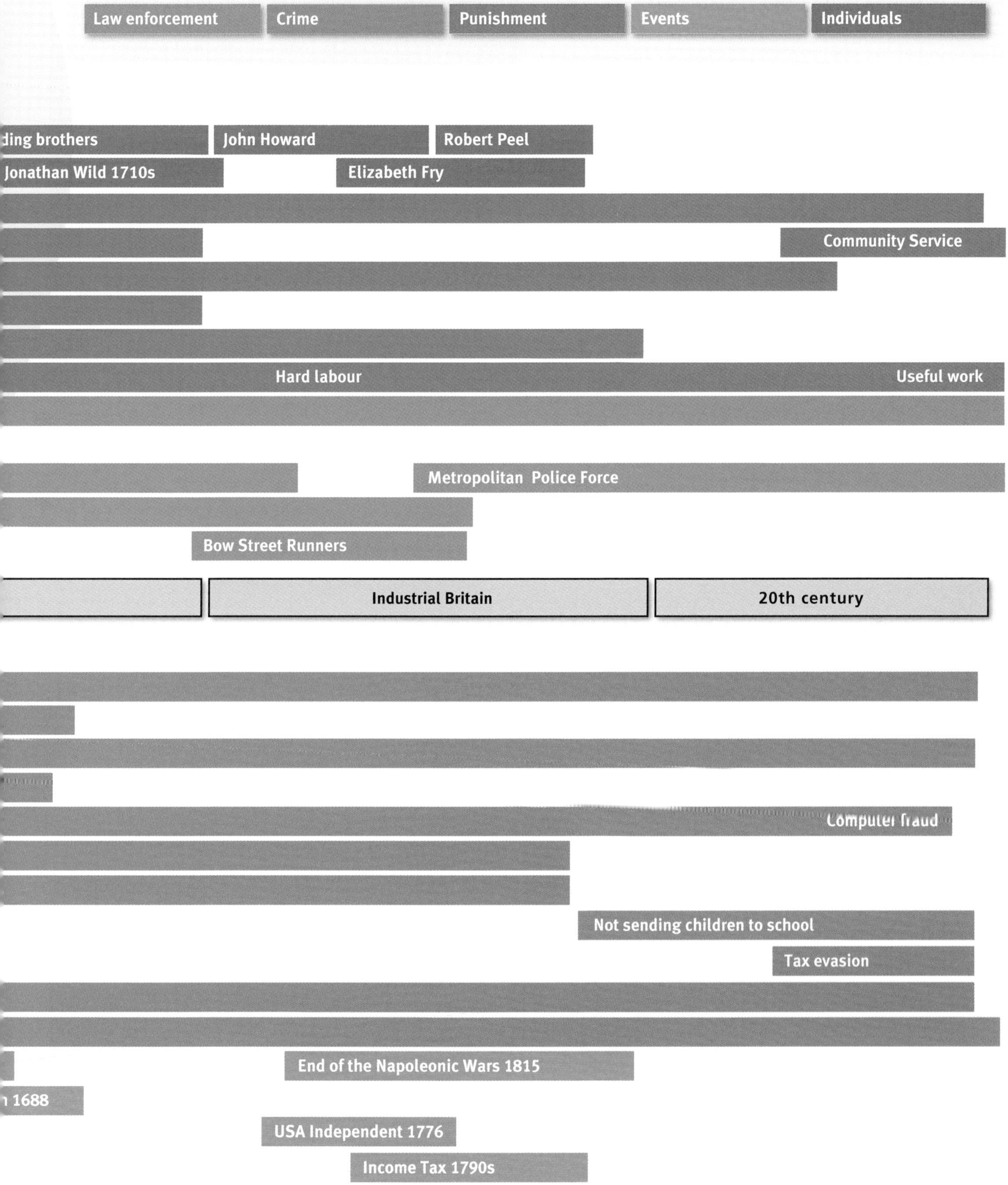
Law enforcement
Crime
Punishment
Events
Individuals
ding brothers
John Howard
Robert Peel
Jonathan Wild 1710s
Elizabeth Fry
Community Service
Hard labour
Useful work
Metropolitan Police Force
Bow Street Runners
Industrial Britain
20th century
Computer fraud
Not sending children to school
Tax evasion
End of the Napoleonic Wars 1815
1688
USA Independent 1776
Income Tax 1790s

Bringing it together – big timeline

You have studied the development of crime and punishment from the Roman period until today, and you have probably seen that the study is part of a complex web of events, individuals and other major factors. This diagram will make sense of the entire study and show you how the various elements sequence, link together and cross over.

Roman law and order

Studying questions and providing answers backed up with evidence are essential skills for all historians. But as well as providing answers to questions set by other people, you can set yourself some questions that can help give an overview of a period or topic that you are studying.

One set of useful questions that you may have come across before are the **5Ws** and **How**. These are:

Who? What? Where? When? Why? How?

These questions allow you to collect together information from various sources and help organise it. One way to use these questions is to look at different themes and answer all of the questions relating to that theme, as has been started below:

Law and order

- Who were the key figures in Roman law and order?
- What changes did they introduce?
- Where did their changes take effect?
- When did their changes come into force?
- Why were these changes needed?
- How effective do you think these changes were?

Crime

- Who were most likely to commit crimes?
- What crimes were seen as the most serious by the Roman Empire?

ACTIVITIES

1. Copy all of the different words and phrases (e.g. hunting, smuggling, USA Independent 1776, etc.) on to coloured sticky-notes or cards (if you haven't got coloured paper then just create your own key so the different sections make sense, e.g. all cards with 'law enforcement' could have a police helmet on them). Mix them all up and then try to piece them together along the timeline.

2. Look at the diagram and consider these questions:
   a. Why did some crimes disappear? Why did some crimes transform into new versions of that crime?
   b. How and why did the purpose of punishment change over time?
   c. What events influenced the discussion about policing?

- Where were crimes most likely to happen in the Roman Empire?
- When did religious crimes change?
- Why were some killings seen as acceptable by the Romans?
- How differently were conquered people treated compared to Romans?

Punishment

- Who?
- What?
- Where?
- When?
- Why?
- How?

ACTIVITIES

1. See if you can come up with questions to ask about the Punishment theme.

2. Another way is to work in pairs. One of you takes the Who, What and Where question categories, the other takes the When, Why and How question categories.

   You each have to come up with three specific questions for each of your question categories. Remember, the idea here is to come up with an overview of the Roman period, so you'll need to think about law and order, crime and punishment when asking your questions.

   Once you both come up with all your questions, it is time to get some answers! You now need to answer your partner's questions – remember to use evidence to back up your answers.

   Now combine your questions and answers with your partner's. You should have the start of an overview that brings together law and order, crime and punishment in the Roman period.

Saxon law and order

The law and order system of Saxon England was a complex one, with many different types of courts and punishments, and responsibility for keeping the peace shared out between many different groups in society.

To get a sense of how the Saxon system of law and justice worked, you might find it useful to draw the information together in a table.

An Anglo-Saxon king and his witan dispensing justice.

ACTIVITIES

1   Go back through the sections that deal with law, order, crime and punishment during the Saxon period (pages 11–17, 46–47 and 104–105) and use the information to complete a table of crimes like this one.

   • In the 'Responsibility' column you should fill in whose job it was to bring the criminal to justice.

   • In the 'Trial by' column, add the type of court you think the trial would be heard in and also whether a trial by ordeal would be used.

   • In the 'Punishment' column, fill in the different types of punishment used in these cases.

   If you cannot find out what to put in a part of the grid from the information in the book, then put in a type of evidence that might help you fill in the table properly and colour code that box.

Crime	Responsibility	Trial by	Punishment
Treason			
Murder of a free peasant			
Murder of a slave			
Mutilation during an assault			
Theft			
Non-attendance at church			
Cattle rustling			
Runaway slave			

Was there a sensible system at the heart of medieval crime and punishment?

It is often difficult to see how systems fit together, because we only see small parts of it working at various times. However, seeing the big picture is really important for understanding how societies work and whether they are successful.

One way to study this is to create links between the various parts of the system. Below are nine key ideas about crime and punishment in the Medieval period. Create an ideas map by making links between the boxes. It is important to make as many links as you can. Remember to draw a line to show a link between the boxes and write along the line to explain your link.

Hue and cry	**Increased trade**	**Gaol for debtors**
Trial by ordeal	**Outlaws and vagabonds**	**Fines more popular**
Feudal system	**JPs holding Assizes**	**Over-mighty subjects**

Fines were mostly for trade issues

Do you remember the four reasons for punishment in the medieval period?

- To increase wealth of the king
- To keep society stable
- To deter criminals through fear
- To follow the Christian and Church example.

Colour code the nine boxes to show which support each of these reasons.

ACTIVITY

Read through the overview and create a table like the one below where you illustrate what continued from the Middle Ages and what had changed.

Time period	Continuity	Change
Law enforcement		
Crime		
Punishment		

Bringing it together: The Early Modern Period, 1450–1750

How did law enforcement, crime and punishment change during this time period?

Who was in charge of law enforcement and punishment in the country?

Although the monarchy was in charge of creating and enforcing laws, landowners and merchants who were not involved in the royal court began to insist on power-sharing through Parliament. By the end of the period and after bloody conflicts like Wars of the Roses and Civil War, the government came under the control of these two groups.

Why was it so hard to catch me?

Law and order did not transform during this time period and instead carried on much like it had done during the Middle Ages so it was easy to get away with some crimes particularly if you moved around a lot like me! As there was no police force or permanent army villages had to organise their own law enforcement like they had in the past so Hue and cry, as well as the posse comitatus, were still in use. The Justices of the Peace also survived the Middle Ages and they were still supported by constables, a Norman invention, and watchmen (first used in 1285) in towns. Thief-takers appeared in many larger towns.

How did criminals like me get punished?

There were many types of punishments that continued from the Middle Ages or earlier, like whipping, mutilation, fines, pillory and stocks. The Tudors also brought back hanging, drawing and quartering! Capital punishment came much more widely used, e.g. the Black Act in 1723 added 50 new crimes to the list and by 1820 you could get executed for almost any crime. Guess what happened to me? You have already studied the use of execution for many crimes, also known as the Bloody Code, and landowners were at the heart of the decisions for this punishment. Transporting criminals started to be used for some crimes, leaving the Houses of Corrections for the more persistent offenders or vagrants.

Was crime really that bad during this time period?

Highway robbery was actually a rather new type of crime as the most common crime (up to 80 per cent) was petty theft, just like in the Middle Ages. Violent crime according to evidence from the time period, suggests that it was decreasing although people thought otherwise. Smuggling was also a new crime because of the high import duties placed on some goods by the government. Other crimes that some would say were created by the government, like vagrancy and poaching for instance, became more widespread as wealthy middle classes felt their property rights had come under threat. Cases of witchcraft also increased particularly during the mid-1700s, as a result of constant religious and political change.

How should a crime and punishment museum be organised?

Imagine that you have been given the task of redesigning your local museum. You have been told that you need to make it only about crime and punishment in the period 1750–1900. This is a very exciting period in terms of crime and punishment, so you will need to make some tough decisions about what goes in and what comes out.

Possible exhibit topics

Law and order

The Fielding Brothers – Bow Street Runners
Robert Peel and Metropolitan Police
Detectives appointed

Crime

Murder rates in 1850–1860s
Poverty and crime
Jack the Ripper
Alcohol and crime

Punishment

The Murder Act, 1752
1810 – 222 crimes carry death penalty
Cato Street conspiracy – leaders beheaded
Last public hanging, 1868
Transportation
New prisons and reformers

ACTIVITIES

1 Your task is to create a guide map like the one below to show the route through your new exhibition.

2 Firstly, look at the old map and work out which current exhibits are from the 1750–1900 time period (the more you can keep the better – it will reduce costs!)

3 Next look at the lists on this page and create new exhibits to fit into the gaps. Variety is essential, so make sure that you have something about law and order, crime and punishment.

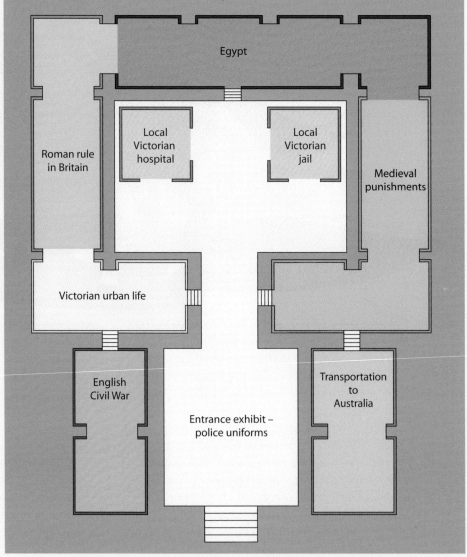

Bringing it together:
The 20th Century

VOICE YOUR OPINION!

According to BBC News, between 6 and 10 million people took part in protests in up to 60 countries over the weekend of the 15–16 February 2003. The government under Tony Blair joined the US war against Iraq in March.

- There have been events in history where the government felt obliged to listen to the public (Poll Tax demonstrations). Should the government have cancelled the attack on Iraq?
- Should a democratically elected government always listen to its people?

ACTIVITIES

Conscientious objection	London bombings 2005	Poll Tax Riots
Sit-in	Hunger strike	Assassination
Rioting	Teachers striking	Hijack plane
Petitioning	Civil disobedience (refusing to obey certain laws)	

The Haydn Protest Continuum
Extremely violent ◀━━━▶ Extremely peaceful

1 Look at the 'protest cards'. Create a similar continuum in your exercise book (or make a living continuum as a class) and place each protest card on the continuum and justify its place. For example, where should 'Rioting' be placed: 'Violent' or 'Peaceful', or maybe somewhere in between? When all 'protests' have been placed, compare with a classmate. Do you agree or disagree?

2 Reorganise your protest cards according to impact on national law and law enforcement, with 'Great change' at one end of the continuum and at the other end, 'No change'. Add these new protests:

- Conscientious objection
- Poll Tax Riots
- London bombing of 2005.

a What forms did the three protests take?

b How does each protest differ?

c How have governments reacted to these challenges to the authority of the state?

ExamCafé

Welcome

You have now completed the Crime and Punishment course. You have got through a lot of content and it is now time to take a step back and make sense of what you have learned.

You now need to revise and prepare for the exams. In this section you will look at the big issues and skills needed to fully understand this Development Study.

Revision is definitely not about reading through the book again the night before the exam. You need to start matching content to specific question types and understand what the examiner is looking for.

You have probably heard this before, but revision is a vital part of the process. You need to think about what has to be learned, how you are going to learn it and then train your brain to make sense of it all.

This Exam Café is designed to help you make connections and understand the exam process. You will learn to be ready for different types of questions and beat the examiners at their own game.

Revision

- Revision checklist
- Ideas maps
- Revision tips.

EXAM PREPARATION

- Sample student answer – practise sources
- Understanding exam language
- Examiner tips
- Planning and structuring an answer
- The Big Idea – expert challenge.

IN THE BEGINNING... Revision Checklist

Before you look at the exam skills it is important that you develop an overview of the content. So, you are going to create a BIG Overview.

Create a massive table covering a whole A4 side (landscape) like this one:

Middle Ages	Early Modern	Industrial	20th Century

Task 1

Below is a large list of words. Write each word in the correct 'era'. You get one mark for each one correct and 2 marks if you can think of the exact date.

Tithing and Hue & Cry	Peterloo
Witchcraft	English Civil War
Glorious Revolution	Matthew Hopkins
Thief-Takers	Rebecca Riots
Bow Street Runners	Bloody Code
Transportation	USA Independent
Elizabeth Fry	Tolpuddle Martyrs
Income tax introduced	End of the Napoleonic Wars
Smuggling	Poaching
The Luddites	Jonathan Wild
John Howard	George O. Paul
Heresy	Metropolitan Police force set up
The Luddites	London Dock Strike
Suffragettes	Guy Fawkes

Task 2

Colour code your words into these categories:

Blue: Law and order
Green: Crime
Black: Individuals
Red: Events

Task 3

Now only look at **Punishments**. Examine the list of punishments below and place them on the timeline you have just created. If a punishment continues e.g. when was hanging used and how long did it continue (ended in 1965…) then draw an arrow across to show that it continued.

Mutilation	Branding
Banishing	Whipping
Stocks/pillory	Fines
Hard labour	Execution/hanging
Transportation	Prison
Community Service	

ExamCafé

Ideas maps
Task 4

Write out each word onto a piece of paper (e.g. one word per A4 or half an A4). Then in groups, or on your own, create a large ideas map on the floor using all the key words. What links can you find between the various events:

- Law and order?
- Crime?
- Punishment?
- Protest?

Get pieces of string and start to make links between points. Add a label to each piece of string to explain what the link is.

Revision tips

Making links is an essential part of revision. Reading something through is rarely enough to make information stick, you need to **do** something with the information. Below are a few tips to help you make the most of revision.

- The most simple approach is 'look, cover, remember' – reading through a short passage and then covering it up and trying to remember as much as you can. This will be even more effective if you have reduced a topic down to a few key points (no more than five).

- Do something unusual with the information: write a song or rhyming poem involving the key points, or create a 3D model that represents the topic (for example, make a box into a prison cell and graffiti the outside walls with reasons for punishments and public attitudes towards it; the inside could be covered in messages about conditions and types of punishment). Make sure that you use a mixture of text and images (images are useful for memory).

- Create a road map for the topic. Create a location to start in the top left-hand corner of a piece of A3 paper (for example, the law and order journey could begin in Justinian City) and then move towards the opposite corner by making a series of roads, obstacles and signs. Be creative: rapid change can become a motorway; changes that faced a lot of opposition can become steep hills to climb.

- Reduce the content down, again and again. Start with your notes and reduce to fifty words. Next make it into three key points. Finally, reduce to three key words. Next, challenge yourself to write about each word for three minutes without looking at your preparation. If you get stuck move up a level and look at your three key points.

ACTIVITY

- Annotate Hogarth's *The Idle Apprentice* using the grid to guide you about:
  - What can you learn about punishment?

HOW TO SUCCEED AT A952

Crime and Punishment A952 is a case-study enquiry with a set of sources which assesses your ability to use sources and develop your own arguments. You will be given a series of sources and need to use these to answer a number of questions. The tasks allow you to work through the sources in carefully managed stages. Do the questions in numerical order. The exam has been set up in a very intelligent way so that you learn to use each source so by the time you reach the last question, which is the most challenging one, you have become familiar with the paper.

Exam Café

Get full marks!

You stand a greater chance of moving up the levels if you know what each question asks of you and if you understand what **Makes a Level** (the Grade Studios in the book will help you with that). Look at the questions below and read each explanation to find out how to best do that:

> **1 Study Source A.**
> Are you surprised that these crimes could be punished by the death penalty? Use the source and your knowledge to explain your answer.
>
> **2 Study Source B.**
> How far does this source give an accurate impression of 18th-century smugglers? Use the source and your knowledge to explain your answer.
>
> **3 Study Source C.**
> Does this source prove that transportation was a failure? Use the source and your knowledge to explain your answer.

Let's take a look at a Question 3 example. Remember that there are several opportunities to practise exam skills throughout the book.

Study Source C.
Does this source prove that transportation was a failure?
Use the source and your knowledge to explain your answer.

[5 marks]

Target: AO1, AO2 and AO3

REMEMBER

No source is ever useless – their unreliability is even useful to historians! Think about these issues **DAMMIT!** (get it?):
Date
Author
Material
Motive
Intended audience
Type of source Or Tone

Level	Description	Mark
0	No evidence submitted or response does not address the question.	0
1	**Uses source to argue it was/was not a failure** This answer will only mention things from the source without supporting with own knowledge. E.g. *'This source does prove it was a failure because it says that prisoners thought Australia was a good place so it would not put them off breaking the law.'* Or evaluates source because of date/secondary.	1–2
2	**Uses source to argue that it was and it was not a failure** These answers will be restricted to information in the source.	3
3	**Contextual knowledge used to argue that it was/was not a failure** E.g. *'No this source doesn't prove it was a failure. As the source says those convicts who had a dreadful time in Australia did not write back home telling people about it. The conditions were terrible. They were put in prison camps like those on Tasmania where they were put to hard labour and were often whipped. They were often put into solitary confinement. So it was not a failure, the convicts were punished.'*	4
4	**Contextual knowledge used to argue that it was and it was not a failure**	5

The Big Idea – Expert Challenge

If you have completed the revision section and followed all the advice you should be ready for the ultimate challenge: arguing with an expert!

On the next page are comments made by the writer Steven Pinker. Look at what he has to say about the violence in society and use your superb knowledge and skills to build up a counter-argument. You do not have to believe in the counter-argument: constructing it is good practice for the interpretation questions in the exam. Also, it will help you to apply your knowledge from the course.

ACTIVITY

What does Source A on page 149 reveal about the state of Britain today?

List five reasons why people might not know their neighbours.

What does this tell you about people's ideas about crime and law and order?

ACTIVITY

Look carefully at the information in Sources A–C on page 149.

What impression of Britain is given?

What do you think people would say about crime and law and order if they were asked in a survey?

Steven Pinker	You
Introduction Genocide, war and violence are everywhere... 'I'm going to present evidence that this particular part of our common understanding is wrong. In fact, our ancestors were far more violent than we are, that violence has been in decline for long stretches of time and that today we are probably living in the most peaceful time in our existence'	**Introduction** Where will you start? What is the opposite of Pinker's view? What popular images of crime and punishment might support this? Why is your argument valid? Give reasons...
First key point: statistical evidence Manuel Eisner, a criminologist gave the following statistics: • There were 100 deaths per 10,000 people in the Middle Ages • There is 1 death per 100,000 people now. Also, there has been a 90 per cent reduction in Genocide since the Second World War	**First key point: statistical evidence** What statistical evidence can you find that disproves this point? How could you explain Pinker's point is not valid?
Second key point: Middle Ages 'Mutilation and torture were routine forms of criminal punishment. The kind of infraction [crime] today that would give you a fine, in those days would result in your tongue being cut out, your ears being cut off, you being blinded, hands being cut off and so on'	**Second key point: Middle Ages** What were the Middle Ages like? Was there any signs of fairness or improvement? Why were punishments harsh? Can you explain this to lessen the impact of Pinker's argument?
Third key point: Early Modern and Industrial Periods 'The death penalty was a sanction for a long list of non-violent crimes: criticising the king, stealing a loaf of bread. Slavery, of course, was the preferred labour-saving device and cruelty was a popular form of entertainment'	**Third key point: Early Modern and Industrial Periods** What were these time periods like? Was there any signs of fairness or improvement? What was changing? Can you explain this to lessen the impact of Pinker's argument?
Conclusion 'The Associated Press is a better reporter of wars on the surface of the Earth than 10th century monks... Things that we read about in the paper with gory footage, burn into the memory more than reports of a lot more people dying in their beds of old age'	**Conclusion** Are our ideas about crime and punishment exaggerated by the media? How could you show that crime and violent crime are rising?

Download Steven Pinker's whole presentation from the TED website, a collection of presentations.

I've got a question for you and I want you to be honest. How many of your neighbours do you know? What about their names? If you know more than five you are doing really well because research shows that fewer than half of us can name between one and five of our neighbours. That's right, most people don't even know five neighbours names!

That didn't come as a surprise to us at The One Show because when we asked about neighbourly spirit on the programme we were inundated with emails from people saying their area had changed for the worse and that people are less friendly than they used to be.

Justin Rowlatt, 'Call yourself a good neighbour?', BBC *The One Show*, 2008.

A selection of weapons collected in an amnesty.

Pensioner attacked in home

A THUG BEAT a pensioner around the head with a clothes hanger in order to steal just £10. The 81-year-old man suffered a sustained attack lasting several minutes after intruders broke into his tower block home in Oldham.

A man and teenage girl slipped into Summervale House on Dale Drive on Friday night and forced open the victim's door.

They then took a two-foot long baton from the wall and repeatedly struck the householder on the head before taking the money.

Source: *Manchester Evening News* website, 7 September 2008.

Glossary

Alms – charity payments made to help the very poor or sick, usually by wealthy people.

Birching – using a thin piece of wood to beat someone.

Black Death – a pandemic disease that spread across Europe from Asia in the mid-19th century. It is estimated that between 30 and 60 per cent of Europe's population were killed.

Bleudfeud – victims getting payment from or revenge on criminals.

Blood money – payment made to a victim's family after a murder.

Capital offence – a crime that was punished by hanging.

Centurian – an officer in the Roman Army.

City-state – an area that is controlled and governed entirely from one city.

Civil liberties – individual rights or freedoms, such as freedom of speech and freedom of religion, which protect ordinary people from government interference. Usually found in democratic societies.

Civil Service – people who carry out duties and administration for the Crown.

Client kings – local leaders who retained power after invasion.

Colony – walled area of land controlled by military veterans from Rome.

Common law – the system of law based on the decisions of the courts and old customs; still used in the legal system today.

Contextual knowledge – knowledge about the period in which an historical event took place.

Crank handle – a useless punishment. Criminals had to turn a handle for most of the day, just to waste their time.

Ealdorman – powerful local leader.

Familiar – in early-modern British superstition, familiars, or imps, were animal-shaped spirits that served witches and demons. They supposedly served as their owners' domestic pets and servants, but also helped bewitch enemies.

Footpad – robber on foot.

Freemen – people who were not slaves or peasants. They did not have to work on the lord's land and were not controlled by him.

Game – any animal hunted for food and not domesticated, for example, deer.

Gemot – people's court.

Gin shop – a shop selling alcohol (gin was the most popular drink at the time).

Governor – Roman appointment in charge of a conquered area.

Impotent poor – people too old or too sick to be able to work.

Industrial Revolution – when a country moves from an agricultural economy to one based on industrial methods of production. Britain was the first country to have an industrial revolution.

Inflation – an increase in the level of prices brought about by an increase in the amount of money in circulation.

Legion – division of the Roman Army.

Magistrate – legal assistant to the Governor.

Medium – person who acts as a link between the living and the spiritual world of the dead.

Misogyny – hatred of women.

Orator – someone to speak in court for the defendant.

Parole – early release from prison for good behaviour.

Patricians – aristocracy.

Penal code – the body of laws relating to crime and punishment.

Plebeians – ordinary people (people not belonging to the ruling class, no matter how much money they had).

Poaching – illegal fishing and hunting.

Poor relief – early local tax where money was raised to support the poor (particularly after the dissolution of the monasteries).

Post-mortem – from the Latin meaning 'after death'; medical examination of a corpse.

Private courts – run by local leaders to deal with minor crimes.

Reeve – royal official.

Regicide – killing of a king.

Royal charter – allowed towns to appoint their own officials and govern themselves.

Senate – political institution.

Servitude – forced labour.

Shire courts – held in each county twice a year to deal with serious crimes.

Social crime – a crime that people generally do not regard as a proper crime.

Socio-economic changes – the relationship between the economy and people's lives.

Sturdy beggars – poor people who could work but refused and begged instead.

Suffrage – the right to vote in elections.

Suffragists/suffragettes – name given to women who campaigned for the vote.

The Bloody Code – the harsh laws that were gradually introduced between 1500 and the 1750s and were punishable by death.

Thralls – slaves.

Treason – betraying one's country or ruler.

Trial by ordeal – deciding whether someone was guilty by using tests that involved pain. It was used if the accused was a suspicious character, had often been accused of crimes or if the jury could not reach a decision.

Tribune – people's court.

Tribune (different definition) – political leader.

Turnpikes – roads with a gate or barrier preventing access until a toll was paid.

Vendetta – taking revenge over a long period for a previous act.

Wergeld – compensation paid to victims after injury at the hands of another.

Witan – this was similar to our Houses of Parliament, where leading figures gathered to give advice on how the country should be run.

WSPU – group set up by leading campaigner Emmeline Pankhurst to actively campaign for votes for women.